DISCOVER THE SECRETS OF

MARKETING THAT WORKS

EXPOSED

Discover The Secrets Of

Marketing That Works

Exposed

———————

47 Time–tested Strategies To Boost Sales,
Get Famous & Put Cash In Your Pockets — Fast!

———————

Michael X. Branson

Strategic Business Guild also publishes its books in a variety of electronic formats. Some content that appears in print may not be available in electronic books and visa versa. For more information about the Strategic Business Guild, visit our website at StrategicBusinessGuild.com

National Library of Australia Cataloguing–in–Publication entry:

Branson, Michael X., 1971- author

Discover the Secrets of Marketing That Works: 47 Time–tested Strategies To Boost Sales, Get Famous & Put Cash In Your Pockets — Fast! / Michael X. branson

ISBN-13: 978-0-9925365-0-3 (paperback)

1. Success in Business 2. Marketing 3. Finance, Personal 4. Entrepreneurship 5.Success – Psychological aspects 6. Quality of life 7. Self–actualisation

CONTENTS

About This Book

When you dig deep, there are two ways to promote and market your business: The stick–a–pretty–ad–somewhere–and–cross–our–fingers approach or a strategically targeted plan to bring in your preferred customer for minimal cost.

The modern approach to marketing creates a substantial advantage for business owners. For the first time since we traded furs for tools and meat, the barriers to successful marketing have crumbled.

Right now, it's actually an advantage to be small. You're nimble, you interact with your customer directly, listening to their wants — and adapting to market demands. The fortune 500's are too big to change direction so quickly. It can take months, even years to plan and make the simplest change to their direction. Like the oil tankers of the sea, they are not going to change directions nimbly like a sail boat. This is your biggest advantage to profit from.

Not only has the Internet become an equalizer by giving thonged entrepreneurs the same tools that are available to big brands and major companies, but it has shifted what is important when it comes to marketing and promoting, creating an incredible opportunity for us.

Now it takes far less money to get yourself out there. It does take more passion, more personality and more creativity to become a trusted resource and the go-to person, as opposed to the me-too product pusher.

Marketing That Works is a sun-lit buffet of fluff-free ideas, and strategies so you can take advantage of this unbelievable opportunity, whether you are a local business owner, entrepreneur, solopreneur, freelancer, or forward thinker ready to innovate and grow.

You must stop trying to out-spend and instead time to out-educate, out-hustle, out-give, out-connect, out-care, out-inspire, out-create, and out-help the competition.

INTRODUCTION

When you break it all down, there are two ways to promote and market your business: throw money at media companies or educate, inspire and become the go-to person in your industry.

Throwing money at media companies is essentially the way it has always been taught: Your job as an entrepreneur, business owner, or marketer is to get as many people as possible to buy by shoving whatever you've got down their throats.

Perhaps your product is the cheapest, the most expensive or the most ordinary (which I'm sure yours isn't). Or perhaps your services are the best in the world. You realize, of course, that a product isn't just limited to a physical entity like a stick figure family for your car or something of the sort. It is whatever someone else wants. It can be services, software, virtual material, yourself (as in the service/ expertise you might provide in a given field), donations . . . whatever.

The thing is, product pushing is crazy expensive. It can be rather pricey to buy traditional ads, hire spokespeople, work with PR and marketing firms still stuck in the '80s, and so forth; so this expense meant mass appeal was the way to go. Cast a wide net and see what you can drag in. Potential customers were everywhere. And if they didn't need your product, the strategy was to create a need and sell, sell, sell. Coke is It, right? Those who had the means and a mega marketing budget were assumed to be the most impressive.

Or you could hire a spokesperson or PR rep and hope your product was interesting enough for some delicious media attention that would encourage people to buy. Or hey, how about a website? You design a website for which the goal is to convince browsers to buy, buy, buy. Or you position yourself within social media and broadcast your message (as opposed to being helpful) with the same end in sight: Sell, sell, sell.

This didn't provide much opportunity for entrepreneurs and forward thinkers like us. Goliaths had the advantage, not the Davids.

But here's the thing and chances are you already know this: We have all gotten wise to the product pushing and are actively repelled by it. Unless you have a marketing budget with a TON of zeros, it can get frustrating.

There has to be a better way, right?

The answer is the marketing that works approach (who saw that coming?). As opposed to product pushing, this method is based around becoming a trusted resource, an authority figure, someone who others like and trust. Not someone who talks down to potential customers but someone who brings people together by being helpful.

The marketing that works approach includes creating (or getting involved with in other ways) valuable content (text, video, audio, and/or speeches/workshops), both online and off, that is focused on educating, inspiring, and/or entertaining. It also means that you have to focus on one–on–one relationship building (off and on line) with a mentality of giving, and in many cases you can use your content as a handshake. It is a change in focus from leading with your product to leading with you.

This new–school approach isn't about becoming a better marketer but instead redefining how we look at marketing and promoting. Because this type of marketing and promoting doesn't taste or look like marketing and promoting (you know, that "ewww" feeling) but instead builds trust, relationships, and you guessed it: sales.

This goes way beyond just creating content. It extends to everything you do and how you approach business and marketing — especially in this increasingly transparent business world where people can reach hundreds or thousands or millions of people with a click of a button (thank you, social Web!).

Because if you think about it, everything is marketing in some shape or form (explicitly or implicitly). Forming relationships with others is essentially marketing yourself. Customer service is marketing because in the social Web age, good AND bad experiences are shared instantaneously. Allowing people to get to know you is marketing. Helping people is marketing. Your online reputation is marketing. What are people saying about you? Who you associate with and who knows you is marketing.

This new era of business creates all kinds of unique opportunities when it comes to marketing, PR, and even rethinking advertising (the big "A" word and, yes, there ARE ways to use marketing that works).

What You'll Get Out of Marketing That Works

The idea here is to spark your imagination. It's to help you tap into your creativity by learning what successful, unique people who have shared their secrets, struggles, and tips do. Of course, the end goal is to take action. Without action, we just have a bunch of ideas in our head (or in a book).

Do you have to do everything in this book to be successful? C'mon now, you know the answer to that. My aim is merely to share with you ideas, real–world examples, and personal experiences from which to draw. I'm not saying you shouldn't spend a million dollars on TV ads for your business if that is what you want to do; by all means, go for it! I am saying there is a new way to market and promote businesses (and yourself) that is just coming of age and now is an amazing time to join this movement.

The bottom line is that our consumers, clients, customers, and friends are all smart, and the changes in marketing happening right now are going to position us and our businesses for success now and way into the future. You are forming long–term relationships (and repeat sales) as opposed to a one–night stand. It's amazing and saddening how many businesses use the one–night stand model.

Why am I telling you this? Honestly, because with enough passion, determination, and willingness to be yourself AND build a business — which pretty much anyone can do — and you can do it in your own way. It doesn't take a Richard Branson. It doesn't take some kind of rocket scientist tech genius. It doesn't take someone of a certain age or personality type. Sure, some will fail, but not us. Not the hustling innovators and forward thinkers who genuinely care.

Sure, this is a book about business. However, it's not an old–school business book, or one whose goal is to convince you how amazing the Internet is, or a personal brag fest of I–did–this–and–you–should–do–exactly–what–I've–done–or–you–are–dumb. There are no charts or graphs, no stuffy case studies, and no complicated "higher math." This is a book filled with ideas, stories of successes and failures, advice from trusted resources, and a buffet of marketing options that come from the perspective and experience of successful entrepreneurs. Hopefully, it is as entertaining as it is informative, and hopefully, you'll find some interesting marketing strategies (as much as I hate that word) that will work well for you and your business. (Then again, you might only read one chapter and regift the book or use it as a paperweight.) Either way...

I hope it proves useful in some manner.

Who This Book Is For

Supershort answer: You.

Short answer: Forward thinking entrepreneurs, freelancers, solopreneurs, savvy marketers, and business owners looking to innovate. Not just survive, but thrive. Be the best.

Long(er) answer: Anyone who has something to promote and market, and is willing to think differently. And it can be ANYTHINGreally. It can either be an existing or future product. It might even be that you are interested in marketing yourself. Perhaps you already know what passion you want to turn into a business and you aren't sure how you will make money from it yet. Or maybe you're promoting services, doing advertising and sponsorships, or attracting investors. Whatever it is, this is for you.

Let's begin by assuming that your products and/or services are amazing (after all, I don't think anyone starts a company or creates a product with the goal of making something ordinary). Because even the most amazing and creative marketing in the world doesn't make up for crappy stuff. If, at the end of the day, your product or service doesn't work or deliver, then marketing that works will sink it just as fast as it could make it rise.

It doesn't matter if you are a pro at marketing and promoting or just getting going. Nor does it matter if marketing and promoting keeps you up at night with excitement because you love it or you cry yourself to sleep because you hate it. There is value at every level. Marketing That Works is designed for forward thinkers. both young and young–at–heart. And it doesn't matter if you are a tech expert or tech confused.

Maybe you've started your tenth company or are thinking about starting your first. Or maybe you're thinking about innovating within your business and rolling out a new product, idea, or service. Perhaps you are a freelancer who stuck it to the man and is now out hustling and building your own business. You might simply be trying to grow your business or look for an edge.

Perhaps you're looking to build a brand that lasts; are a personal brand or "solopreneur" looking to generate more business; or (omg!) a big brand looking to think different. Or you are a marketer who has noticed that your target market seems to have dried up. Where the heck did they go and how do you reach them?

Now, who is this book NOT for (an equally important distinction)?

Anyone looking for a get rich quick scheme. This book isn't for you, so please hand it to someone else. Established business and marketing principles have been around for decades and building businesses and brands today still takes hard work, patience, dedication, resilience, risk, and a bit of luck (okay, sometimes a lot of luck). While building trust is key, it is based upon the idea of nimbleness and creative hard work — as opposed to an easy way out. No way around it: It takes time to be successful in the modern market.

This book is not for those looking for an exact road map or a how-to book. Why? Because there is no single road map. In fact, this is why we are all entrepreneurs — we want to make our own maps, right? If there's one thing learned from personal experience, hundreds of interviews, and tons of conversations, it's that entrepreneurs like to learn and do things differently. If you tell us what to do, we'll nod politely then do it our own way.

HOWEVER, if you share experiences, stories, and lessons with us, we can pick out the juicy bits to use for our business. This book is meant to be a source of ideas and inspiration based on real life as opposed to fluffy bunny theories taught by someone who hasn't experienced it. Some things will work for you, and others may not but I can promise that everything here is based on experience, success and failures, both my own and others'.

This book is not for naysayers. You know the type. They are the ones who, when it is 23 degrees and sunny, complain that it isn't 24 degrees.

Naysayers find the worst in everything. The glass isn't even half empty, it's not worth drinking out of at all. They're often characterized by a lack of wanting to try new things, and are fixated on the way things were. They always have excuses aplenty.

WHAT YOU CAN EXPECT

The big ideas and principles in this book aren't arrived at by simply throwing sand at passers-by and hoping some of it sticks. I've analysed the big guns over the past five years. I've spoken to big-time entrepreneurs, creative thinkers, unique business people, outrageous marketers. In short, people who are living their passion every day, are massively successful, walk the walk and talk the talk. These are people we can learn from because they really have tasted it. Because learning from the best is always a great way to be inspired (and then you can always do it your own way if you prefer).

Now is the time to take that sand and build castles to attract, inspire and create conversations on how they can build their own dream castles too.

Without further ado, let's get our hands sandy...

PART ONE: THE FOUNDATIONS

WHAT YOU NEED TO KNOW TO MAXIMIZE THESE
PROVEN MARKETING STRATEGIES

---

1. SUCCESS IS UP TO YOU

"Insanity: doing the same thing over and over again and expecting different results."

Albert Einstein

You want things to change? Do you? Really?

It's awesome that you've picked up this book, looking for a way to improve your business, your life and your hip pocket and yet there might be unrealized limiting beliefs which are sapping your strength and sabotaging your efforts.

Preparing your mind for success is the first step on the path to greater profits in your business in the new economy. In fact, I'll even go a step further and predict that unless you address your mindset first, you won't even implement a single one of the proven strategies in this book or make any extra cash.

Think this sounds a bit harsh? Well, would you rather me sugar coat it and skim over the meat and potatoes or would you rather sit down and have a seven course meal that will have you bursting at the seams with ready–to–buy, customers and profits?

No matter how great the strategies are that I reveal within the pages of this book, you will never see one extra cent of profit unless you are willing, ready and able to make the changes required. And that, my friend, requires guts, boldness and the ability to move rapidly to follow the money in your local market.

Let me give you few examples of how powerful and profitable OR how broke and hungry a mindset can make you. There's a successful fashion store in Sydney which promises delivery in 3 hours or less. Do you have an idea of the average amount of days or weeks a customer was accustomed to waiting to get their clothing delivered before this company decided to rewrite the rules? Normal delivery wait time was two to six weeks for in stock merchandise. In fact, I would venture to say that 95% of the fashion industry still requires customers to wait two to six weeks for delivery. This turn–the–industry–on–its–head fashion store has a huge competitive advantage over every other fashion store in their marketplace.

Now, before this fashion store came to the area, no other stores were even delivering clothes to a customer's office within a couple of days let alone 3! Do you think these owners were scorned and warned by ALL the other fashion retailers who they asked for advice? Do you think manufacturers, vendor reps and delivery companies scoffed and swore that it couldn't be done? Of course! Every fashion store has the same problems and objections as any other, but the owners of this fashion chain believed that they could do it better and faster.

The owners of that company had the iron resolve of Winston Churchill. They had a powerful mindset that allowed them to grow beyond belief... During a recession! However, they first had to change their mindset BEFORE they could ever change their business. That's what you will also have to do in order to grow your business to the next level.

Now, let's look at how badly things turn out when business owners have a stubborn and poor mindset. Several years ago there were several super-high end fashion stores within miles of each other in Sydney. These retailers were priced so high, that only two percent of the population in the entire nation could afford their fashion. As the economy turned, those retailers simply refused to change their business model to reflect the change in the economy. Therefore, within six short months ALL but one of those retailers went out of business.

Unfortunately, the stubborn and poor mindset also affected many others who could have easily weathered the storm of this economy with just a few simple changes to their businesses. They chose to ignore the changing marketplace and consequently went out of business.

Now that you know how powerful a mindset change is to your success, let's look at four powerful realities that you must embrace to weather any economy:

1. Accept that there's still money in your local marketplace. Don't feed me that garbage that people in your area aren't buying the type of products or services that you offer. Yes, they are. There are dozens of businesses who are making unbelievable profits during this recession. The real question is "Will yours be one of the businesses that will make the necessary changes in order to cash in during an economic downturn?"

2. Take advantage of the opportunities that recessions create. Every recession creates an opportunity for someone to profit. In the example of the fashion store chain that I mentioned earlier, consumers want fashion delivered quickly that they could wear that night. The customers in that market don't want to wait for months. They want good price, speed and convenience. Ultimately, the key to your success will be determined by your ability to listen to your market. Then, all you have to do is create a product or service to meet that need and you'll instantly attract more profits.

3. Make decisions based on numbers, not 'opinions'. If you're listening to talk radio, news reports and any other media source that's pumping fear, doom and gloom into your head, then turn it off right now! The majority of news media sources are in the business of selling fear, not hope. Your focus should be on finding what your target market wants and then giving it to them at a great value. That's it. Don't let the media drive you out of business, by slowly draining away your will to fight.

4. You're either green and growing or ripe and rotting. Every day I meet so many business owners who simply refuse to do things differently, but yet, they expect different results. That's the textbook definition of insanity. You must be willing to change your staff, advertising, marketing, product, management, and everything else, in order to survive during this new economy. That's the truth, plain and simple.

Set aside any preconceptions of what works or doesn't work and look at each with a fresh mind with the intent to seriously apply it. You will begin to notice that each of these strategies has been used before. In fact you will see some of them again and again in your letter box, on your TV, online and in your newspaper. If each of these other businesses are willing to spend the cash over and over again on that strategy, you can be damned sure they're making a profit with them.

You can too.

2. The Five Keys to Creating a Cash Focused Marketing Plan

While taking your mindset to the next level in your business is the first step towards transforming your business into a marketing machine, there are several other key principles which will greatly impact your success. These five factors are so important to your business success in this new economy, that unless you build your marketing strategies using them, you will have a 98% chance of failing. Take your time with these five keys.

Key #1: Know your Numbers

When business owners hire me to help turn their business into a money–maker, one of the first things I do is have them complete the Business Lifeblood Formula. The Business Lifeblood Formula takes into account the entire marketing and sales process and gives you five essential points to measure and improve your business.

The Business Lifeblood Formula is:

Leads

x Sales Conversion

= Customers

x Average Transaction Value

x Transaction Frequency

= Revenue

x Margin

= Profit

Each of these five are points in your marketing and sales process that even if you only improve each of them by 15%, you can double your profits! Let me show you how.

These five points help you determine the three critical values that will help you decide which marketing program produces the most profit for your business... And which ones need to change or drop.

With these five points in hand you can now discover the three growth metrics of your business. They are the CPC, LV and the CoCR of your customers.

The CPC or Cost Per Customer is the amount you spent to get them in the door and make a purchase. The less you need to spend to get the customer the better. BUT there is a strategic advantage to spending more than your competitors can afford to IF and only IF your customers Lifetime Value is high enough to justify it and you have the cash available upfront.

The next is the LV or Lifetime Value of your customer. This is the amount they are reasonably expected to give you over the course of their buying lifetime with you. We want this to increase as much as possible. It is also worth segmenting your customers to see just how much certain groups are worth - and why you must foster better relationships and attract more high LV groups into your business.

The CoCR is the Cash on Cash Return. With this, you KNOW that for every dollar you spend you will reasonably expect to get back X dollars in profit.

Lets look at some examples to help you see the importance of the Business Lifeblood Formula.

The numbers below list each of the five points with dollar values for a small business:

1. Leads 7500

2. Conversion Rate 20%

Customers 1500

3. Frequency of Sales 2

4. Average Sale Value $125.00

Total Revenue (Customers x Sales x Sale Value) ....
.... $375,000.00

5. Margin 25%

Profit (Revenue x Margin) $93,750.00

Marketing Investment $20,000

Lifetime Value (Profit / Customers) $62.50

Cost Per Customer to acquire (Marketing Investment/ Customers) $2.67

Cash on Cash Return % (LV / CPC x 100) 2344%

In this example each customer (on average) costs you $2.67 (CPC) to get and returns you $62.50 (LV) in profit over their purchasing lifetime. This gives you a Cash on Cash Return of 2344% or $23.44 for every $1 you invest.

How many times are you willing to spend $1 to have $23.44 put back in your pocket?

It doesn't have to stop there. In fact, your next goal should be to improve each of the five profit points:

1. Leads

2. Conversion Rate

3. Frequency of Sales

4. Av. Sale Value

5. Margin

The reason why each of these points are so important is because they show you the profitability of your business and provide confidence in how much you should invest in marketing to get the customer in the first place.

Looking at the example above, the business owner (you) knows that if you spend another $20,000 marketing in the same ways you are investing in now, you can reasonably expect to double your profits. Without knowing the Cash on Cash Return, you wouldn't have the confidence to make that kind of investment in marketing.

What if you weren't that confident about doubling your marketing? What if you just focused on each of the five points and improved them just a little, say 10%. In reality 10% is a very achievable improvement. How would this affect your bottom line?

Let's find out.

Adding 10% to each of the five points below:

1. Leads **8250**

2. Conversion Rate **22%**

Customers 1815

3. Frequency of Sales **2.2**

4. Average Sale Value **$137.50**

Total Revenue (Customers x Sales x Sale Value) ....
....$549,037.50

5. Margin **28%**

Profit (Revenue x Margin) $150,985.31

Marketing Investment... $20,000

Lifetime Value (Profit / Customers) **$83.19**

**Cost Per Customer to acquire (Marketing Investment/
Customers)** **$2.42**

Cash on Cash Return (LV / CPC x 100) **3431%**

How did you do it? By using your marketing dollars smarter, you gained an extra 750 leads. You also changed the headline for 10% more conversion but that's ok. By adding an upsell, the Average Sale Value went up and you found a way to increase your margin by 10%. You also sent a special invitation to your customers for a private sale and 10% of them showed up, increasing the frequency.

What happened? Profits are up, Customers bought more frequently. It cost you less to get each lead in the first place and you now get $34.31 for every dollar you spend!

That's a whopping 61% improvement in your pocket!

Do you still think 10% is too much? What if you only focus on improving one of the five by 1% every week. You can do that right? In fact it wouldn't take much to make that happen using the strategies you now have in your hand. You can have two weeks off and still achieve that 61% improvement in the next 12 months.

Would an extra $75,000 make a difference in your business? Don't make excuses, make profits.

Using this formula you can also measure a marketing campaign. Take the measured data from the campaign and work out the Frequency of Sales based on what an average customer does purchase over a year.

You can only improve what you measure.

The important thing is to have a customer value and profit expectation you can use to compare different marketing strategies and the health of your business over time.

Ok. Let's stop for a minute. Grab a piece of paper or your journal. Record your numbers. Later on, you can record the new numbers as you apply the different strategies in this book. You might be surprised at how much a customer is really worth to you and why it's so important to be building a stronger relationship with them.

Key #2: Know Where They Came From

"Half the money I spend on advertising is wasted; the trouble is I don't know which half"

John Wanamaker, 1922

If there was one piece of advice that I would want you to remember from this entire book, it would be tracking where every lead comes from and how to contact them again. Every Ad, every phone call, every email enquiry should be recorded and analysed.

In order to track where your leads came from, you can ask them when they walk into your business or you can use special phone numbers in your ads. You can use simple five page websites designed for a specific sale. Even customized coupons for each media, unique tracking codes or anything else you can think of to help you know exactly where they came from.

When you know where they came from, you can track the effectiveness of each ad, how profitable they are and which needs improving. Once you know where your leads are coming from, you can also begin to invest more marketing in those specific areas that are generating the best leads and customers.

Different groups of people respond differently to different offers in different media. Tracking helps you turn your opinion into measurable results.

Without tracking your leads, you will always be wasting thousands of dollars on ineffective marketing strategies — and you won't even know where.

Key #3: The Money is in Your List. Seriously.

You've run your numbers. It might be costing you $50 to get a customer. It sort of makes you cringe doesn't it? What if you could reduce that cost–of–sale to, say, $0. You'd be grinning like a Cheshire cat wouldn't you?

If they had only ever bought once before, and you send them an offer via email tailored just for them, can you see how that is an instant $50 profit increase? You're no longer paying to market to them. Right?

Why do so many businesses continue to ignore them and their goodwill (you did make them happy right?) to only focus your time on finding new customers, spending $50 again and again? Sounds silly right? Well 97% of you are doing just that and I'm here to put a stop to it.

Seriously, record every one of your customers contact details in a database and track every contact you have with them. How much they spend, how frequently they shop, their address, email, mobile. Everything.

Now, send them offer after offer for different products and services that they find interesting so that 1) they know what other services you offer and 2) You tempt them to buy again and again.

How may offers? That depends on your business offerings, your customers buying habits and your ticket price. You're not going to get multiple car purchases in a year from the average person (but then you wouldn't target them would you?) but you are going to get multiple repeat sales from a pizza shop and even an extra one or two sales for a car service center.

If your business burns down and all you have is your list, you can get cash coming in almost immediately, helping to get back up and running. Gloria Jean's did in their early days. Peter Irvine talks about how they survived on customer and supplier goodwill and you can too.

How do you build your list?

There's many ways to build a list that fall into the following strategies:

- Ask
- Run a competition
- Privileged Club
- Continuity program
- Newsletter
- Record the Sale

Ask: Nothing can be simpler. High priced and service businesses already have names and contact numbers; just ask for the rest. A doctors practice I know simply states "its policy" when questioned.

Run a Competition: Competitions are a great way to collect contact details and most people understand that you'll send something in the future. If it's highly valuable information or an awesome offer it'd be welcomed and they won't opt out.

Privileged Club: The sooner you can start a premium service or club, the better. There is always someone willing to pay top dollar for personalized service and even more willing to fork out a few dollars a year/quarter/month to get exclusive discounts and prioritization.

There was a club around town that was the "in" place to be. On Fridays there was always a queue to get in the front door. The owner was a smart cookie and creatively offered to sell a $200 VIP program so you could go and line up out the back. Toss in a few fast expiry drink vouchers and soon enough, the line out the back ended up longer than the front! As with all clubs, the "in" crowd moved on and they closed down but the concept is easily repeatable in any arena.

You can see this system used in conferences, hotels and airports all over the world. Because it works.

Another similar way to collect information is in Birthday Clubs. Reward your customers with a free meal or something appropriate on their birthdays — all for the privilege of receiving special offers every month to bring them back, spending with you more frequently. After all if you have an expiring voucher for a discount in business X, why would you shop in business Y? Look at how Coles has now dominated the Australian mind. Woolworths used to be the top marketer and now they're forced to play catchup.

Continuity Programs: Having continuity programs is also the fastest way to get a known amount of cash every month before you even lift a finger!

The biggest example is ProActiv skincare. They use celebrity endorsements carefully chosen to attract their target demographic (know your customers!) and they only sell via a monthly auto-billing program. That auto-billing program tells them exactly how much stock they need and how much profit they will make... all before even shipping a single box. Coupled with their Cost per Customer and their conversion rate, they know how much they will make next month and even next year to a fair degree of certainty.

How does this apply to you? Can you offer a maintenance program with your products? What about an auto-shipping refill service?

Newsletters: They are a great tool to keep the customer engaged, build a list and demonstrate that you are the go-to person for your niche.

A newsletter should be about giving value to the customer. Great content for newsletters can be featured customer stories, value adding how-to's, staff highlights, life events and anything else people like to know about people. That isn't to say you'd show off your new boat or Aston Martin. Keep it about the people. Kids, weddings, pets antics. Anything interesting you'd like to share. Include your customers, highlight one and talk about what they are doing, how they used your product and generally showing how great they are. Don't forget to mention your next sale event but keep it conversational and don't make the newsletter about it.

Record the Sale: Every sale you make should contain enough information to be able to contact them again. The higher the price point, the more information you should already have. Start with that and use the other five to fill in the blanks as your price point drops.

That's six ways you can start building a list. You can mix and match or do all six. They all work and the purpose is to build that list so you can connect, build a relationship and grow your profits.

Key #4: Create Ads and Marketing Materials that Consistently Put Money in Your Pocket

Going global for a minute, if you ever want to see a huge waste of money, watch the ads being played during the American Super Bowl. Those ads that run during the Super Bowl are designed to be funny, cute and win advertising awards. They cost obscene millions of dollars yet those ads rarely make their companies any real profit. As a matter of fact, those commercials are the laughing stock of the true marketing industry because these companies blissfully line up and pay those millions for those types of "funny" ads while receiving little to no results for their marketing dollars.

The fact of the matter is you either need to learn how to write and design effective ads or have the smarts to hire a good copywriter. Regardless of which option you choose, I encourage you to learn about copywriting so that you have a feel for what usually works. As the owner, you should definitely know how to create ads, letters and emails that generate leads. To get you started, here the core elements which every ad you create should have:

- Headlines that attract specific customers.

- A compelling, irresistible offer.

- Use a specific start date and deadline in your ad.

- Insert testimonials from past customers.

- A strong guarantee on your offer.

- Look unique and stand out from your competitors.

- ONLY focus on what your customer wants.

- Have only one action goal for each ad, whether it's to visit, call or send in an order.

- Explain the reason why you're offering the sale.

- Write ads that are straight to the point and easy to understand. Don't use long, three syllable words if you can.

- Write to woo their emotions, not their logic.

The great Dan Kennedy (copywriter extraordinaire) wrote once that you should include these points in your copy:

- Agitate Pain

- Remove Blame

- Relieve Fear

- Encourage Dreams

- Confirm Suspicions

- Help Them against Their Enemies

Don't rely on just one ad for your marketing; always be testing it with different headlines and offers.

I learned about an ad that out-pulled everything it was put against because of a simple printing mistake that was just brilliant! The printers changed 'Get' to 'Gets' and it converted 23% better. Track, measure and test everything. Use the best responsive ad as the control to beat and try something new. You never know what your customer responds best to unless you try it. If you use photos in your ad, rotate them around. People get used to seeing the same ad and start ignoring it. It's called ad blindness and can cost you dearly.

Key #5: When Everybody Is Your Customer, Nobody Is.

One of the biggest challenges business owners must overcome in order to be successful in this new economy, is the dreaded "I-offer-everything-for-everyone" syndrome. On the surface this seems like a sure-fire way to get more customers, but it's been proven time and time again that it's not always the most successful way to prosper for 99.9% of you. Let's examine it a little closer.

If you're a small business owner, then chances are that you have a limited budget and limited space to work with.

Let's say for example that you're a furniture store. If your store offers several contemporary collections, several ultra-modern collections and some eclectic pieces as well as some early Colonial collections scattered throughout your business.

Do you really think you have enough of any single style to satisfy the type of customer who's looking for a specific style? The answer is most likely no.

In fact, the most successful furniture retailers in an area focus on a couple of things to attract a specific type of customer, such as (pick two or three):

- Specific styles popular in the area.

- Complete living room packages for under $2,000 or furnish your entire home for under $5,000.

- Long–term low or no interest financing

- Fast delivery within 3 days or less

- Lower prices for packages

- Higher quality and levels of service

By narrowing down their advertising, they can attract the types of customers who will purchase multiple pieces and drive the average ticket sale and profits up. They then offer generous financing terms, which attracts customers with good credit and income, while enticing them to spend more money because the customer has longer to pay for it. Most importantly, the successful retailers price their sales so that the more merchandise the customer buys, the bigger the discount the customer receives.

Please remember it's not always about the price. While a lot of these examples are written for the more normal businesses, there are a lot of wealthy clients where quality, exclusiveness, prestige, value and service are foremost. If you can offer a premium level to them, and package it accordingly, you will be amazed at how profitable you will be.

There is also another twist to these retailers. Although they attract customers to their business with generous financing offers, they reward their salespeople handsomely for NOT selling the long-term financing, therefore giving their salespeople an incentive to get customers to pay off their balances in less than 30 days. And these are just a few of the strategies that successful businesses use to attract customers without focusing exclusively on price.

I like to say "The Loot's in the Lair". Simply put, this means that you need to determine who your most profitable, enjoyable and easy to attract customer is and where they 'hang out', then specialize in getting more of those customers to come into your business to buy.

People like to associate with people like themselves. If you have a profitable subgroup of customers, shouldn't you be trying to get more just like them? Where's their lair? Online forums? Social Clubs? Magazines or particular newspapers? Find it and learn what makes them tick, what causes them to reach for their wallet? Then use it in your marketing!

3. STANDING OUT FROM THE CROWD

The best way to stand out from the crowd and attract your preferred customer is to use a strategic positioning catchphrase. A U.S.D. (Unique Selling Distinction) compels your most profitable customer to think of you and come back to your business again and again. The U.S.D. is the wow factor that you're known for. It is also the promise to the customer.

Let's look at a few examples:

- "When it absolutely, positively has to be there. Overnight"

- "Fresh, piping hot pizza delivered to your door in 30 minutes or it's free"

- "The milk chocolate that melts in your mouth, not in your hand"

- "We try harder"

- "Just do it"

- "Diamonds are forever"

- "Good to the last drop"

- "The other white meat"

- "We get you"

The first three of these stand out immediately and tell you exactly what to expect from the company — and how you benefit. They are great examples of U.S.D's.

The rest are brand driven and require constant repetition to associate the slogan with the company. Sure they convey a message and position the company but do they really convey what the customer wants from them?

Which ones tell you what you'll get and would compel you to use that company when you want their product? Which type of slogan do you think you should you be using? A strong offer driven U.S.D.? Or a brand supporting slogan? I know you picked the first one right?

Developing your U.S.D.

The first step in developing a U.S.D. is to determine the profile of your most profitable customer. You will want to know things like; how they found your business, where they live, what newspapers and magazines they read, where's their Lair?

Next is to find out what they care about and why they chose you. This is the critical step.

Here's an example of some of the information that you may discover about your prospects and customers:

• Wives initially visited your business without their husbands.

• Recently married

• Has 1 kid

• Plays Tennis

• Drives a SUV

• Reads Gossip magazine

• Uses Facebook Daily

• Lives within five miles of your business

• Spent between $800 – $1500

• Visits 3.7 times a year

• Pays by Amex

Once you have this information, you can refocus your marketing and your business to cater for more of the same types of customers that are currently spending the most money in your business.

However, you can only use this information to your advantage if you take the time to collect it in the first place. You can then dig deep and find out who your customer is, what's important to them, what they hate in your industry (and what you can do about it) and what they truly want.

These 5 keys will change the way you look at your business, get you out of the 'commodity' game and make you the obvious choice for your chosen market. They may seem like a lot of hard work, but you only have to do the hardest work in the beginning. As always, the most important factor which will contribute to your success in your business is your willingness to actually implement these strategies on a consistent basis and track the results.

Because these are so important, I highly recommend that you stop reading any further and go back over each one — and apply it to your business first.

You will gain a deeper understanding of your position in the market, your profitability and the most important areas you need to change in order to break through the barrier of being a 'me–to' business and become a 'market leader' business.

4. Your A.B.S. Plan

"If you fail to plan, you are planning to fail!"

Benjamin Franklin

Always Be Selling. Sounds obvious, doesn't it? But, you wouldn't believe how many business owners I meet who refuse to do any type of consistent marketing or advertising! That is unbelievable to me yet it seems to be normal for many businesses. Sure, they will do a small little ad in the local newspaper once or twice a year, but that can hardly be considered marketing consistently?

If I were to ask you what kind of business you're in, what would you say? If you're like most business owners that ask me for coaching, you would probably just pick a product or service that you sell and simply tell me that you are in that industry.

Well, I'm here to tell you that your answer to the question of what business you're in, should be, "I'm in the marketing business." If that was not your answer, then I already know that you're most likely having huge profit problems in your business.

Many business owners are in confused about what business they are in. The simplest way to look at your business is to realize that the two most important activities in your business is marketing and actually providing the product or service that you're marketing. Every day that the doors of your business are open, is a day that you should be focusing on marketing.

I know business owners are not to blame for being unable to put together an effective marketing campaign. Think about when you first started your business. Did you receive an instruction manual on how to get customers? Was there a course offered down at the local college designed to teach business owners how to attract quality buying customers?

Heck, no. You just went out there and told everyone what you're now doing and then you probably sat back and waited for customers to come into your business. Back then things were pretty easy. That gravy train didn't last, did it?

Next, you probably turned to the industry publications, magazines and newsletters, which focus on products and customer service as the solution to your problems. Over time you looked around at what the competition was doing and you probably began to think that if you also offered product or service at a lower price, customers would flock to your business as well. But, is that what really happened?

Maybe at first you saw a rush of customers the first time you ran a new ad or promotion with the product at a low price, but did it continue on like that? No. As time went on you probably began doing less and less advertising because you weren't seeing the results from you advertising dollars. But deep down inside, you knew that you had to do some type of marketing and advertising, but you had no idea what to do. After all you're a business owner, not a marketing and advertising guy.

That is where you're unfortunately mistaken. If you want to be a successful and profitable business owner, you MUST become a marketing and advertising guy! Your number one job every single day is getting more customers into your business. That's it. Why, you ask? Because the only way you make money is if customers come into your business and are willing, ready and able to pay you cash in exchange for your product or service.

You don't get paid to counsel employees, do payroll, answer questions about when the delivery truck will arrive and you sure as heck don't get paid to sit around all day waiting for someone to walk in. You only get paid when and if a customer pays you.

Your number one job every day when you wake up has to be getting more paying customers through your doors. The only way to do that is to become a marketing and advertising fanatic.

Isn't it exciting when you see a lead walk in, hand you a wad of cash and leave as another satisfied customer?

When you begin to look at yourself as the marketer of your business, instead of just a business owner, it will become very easy to see if you're doing the right things to attract customers or not. I knew business owners who NEVER advertised their business and shortly after the recession hit went belly–up.

In fact, every day you that you seriously want to make money, you should be running a different promotion, ad or marketing campaign. Don't tell me that customers get tired of seeing your ads, because I'm going to tell you to advertise in a different area that hasn't seen that specific advertisement or promotion yet. Don't tell me that it's too expensive, because I know about one hundred ways to advertise your business on a shoe–string budget and most of them cost less than what you spend on lunch for the week.

In order to succeed in this new economy, you MUST view yourself as the marketer of your business and NOT just an owner of your business.

Create your A.B.S. Plan... Right Now!

Do you have a marketing plan? It's OK if you don't because we're here to change that. Most business owners won't be able to weather this economic storm simply because they don't have the foggiest clue where their customers will come from. What promotions they are going to running in the next week, much less in the next month or year!

We can change this so you will survive and thrive in this new economy.

Stress quickly kills creativity and every business has some level of stress to deal with. Imagine knowing what your next campaign's profits will most likely be takes away the stress of not knowing where the next customer is coming from because you've already planned for it!

Now, coming up with a 12 month marketing plan may seem like a daunting task, but most of the work is already done for you. How, you ask? Well, customers are already expecting you to have a special sale or promotion at least once a month on the major holidays. You don't have to recreate the wheel; you can just ride the wave of marketing and advertising messages that are already around that time frame.

While the dates are already set on the calendar, it is still important that you have compelling offers in your advertisements for that specific holiday. Do NOT run a general advertisement that simply says you have stuff on sale. Your ads need to match the holiday theme as closely as possible.

Some sales should be percentage discounts, but some sales should be packages with something given for free in exchange for making a purchase.

The most effective way is to offer something free with the purchase or create a bundled offer only valid for this holiday.

Discounts tend to cheapen your value while giving something for free tends to enhance your value in the customers eyes.

The last and final step is to remember to set up a marketing campaign consisting of several methods of communicating with your prospects. For example, you can send out postcards, letters, emails and pre-recorded phone messages. Most times it takes contacting a customer several times before they can actually make a buying decision.

People always look forward to holidays and when you promote something they want leading up to the holiday, those happy feelings are transferred onto your business making the whole sales process easier and with a stronger associated lifetime value. Just look at all the toy sales leading up to school holidays. We could also argue as to who gets the most benefit. The kids? Or the parents with a happy occupied child during the holidays.

Let's look at 12 monthly holidays you can use in a marketing calendar:

January — New Year's / Australia Day

February — Valentine's Day

March — International Women's Day

April — April fool's / Easter / Anzac Day

May — Mother's Day

June — Father's Day / EOFY / Queens Birthday

July — Fourth of July /Mid-Year School Break

August — No major events = Friends & Family Sale

September — Labor Day

October — Halloween

November — Melbourne Cup / Thanksgiving

December — Christmas / EOY

What promotions can you run on these holidays? What offers would work well with them?

What about international days of interest? There's one for nearly every day of the year. Just Google for International Day {month} and you'll find something to celebrate/support. Remember it's about the event tied in with a compelling and complementary offer, not just a 'sale'. Arrrr! Ye be wanting yer free slurpie then matey? 7-11's Talk Like a Pirate Day promotion won them sales, FREE media exposure and traffic to their petrol stations.

(Your Action Guide starts on the next page)

Take action NOW:

1. Start by selecting the events you want to use in your promotions.

2. Create complementary bundles and offers for those events.

3. Give them promotional names

4. Make a Sale Event Action List (SEAL) of what needs to be done; Ads, media, signage etc.

5. Mark the calendar for the Events

6. Mark the calendar a month or so earlier with the SEAL for the upcoming event.

7. Pull out the next SEAL and get stared!

8. Launch the Event

9. Record the results

You'll find the following years much easier because you've already done the hard work. Just tweak things around based on your Response Metrics, count the cash and get ready for the next one!

With a yearly marketing calendar, you will gain a feeling of confidence and reassurance because you are not just sitting on your hands, day–in and day–out, waiting for customers to just walk in and maybe buy something from you. You KNOW what you have to do for next month's campaign.

5. How to Host a Very Profitable F&F Sale

The Friends & Family Sale has long been used by the retail industry as an advertising tool to generate customers. Unfortunately, I have very rarely seen businesses outside of the retail industry use the strategy.

Why not find a way to make this sale a part of your advertising strategies. After all, the chances are pretty good that your current customers know other people who are similar to them who could use your product or service.

However, before you run out and try this strategy, I must give you a word of caution. Over the years, I have noticed that if you run this sale the wrong way, it runs the risk of being a huge flop.

After investigating and testing in businesses, I found that the large majority of the times when we promoted our friends and family sales, we always got prospects who would have bought days or weeks earlier if we would have just offered them the same deal earlier.

This completely defeats the purpose of having the sale. In fact, we were only risking losing the customer and delaying our profits because we were discouraging them from buying today, so that they could get the better sale price later.

Here's the solution. Create ads that clearly state that the prospect can only get the discount if they bring friends and family with them to the sale. You can even tier the discount to handsomely reward those prospects who bring more friends and family. For example, give a five percent discount if they bring one person, ten percent discount if they bring two, and a fifteen percent discount if they bring three and a whopping twenty percent discount if they bring four people.

However, the key to the entire sale is that the friends and family must fill out a simple little contact information form when they visit you. You can even create a contest that they are being entered into to win prizes. When you let them know why you're gathering the information, they will feel less awkward giving it to you. At the very least, this allows you to build your marketing database, and you may even get a sale or two from them at the sale, but the bonus benefit is that you get to grow your prospecting list.

Finally, make sure the terms of the Friends & Family Sale are well laid out on your website or on the advertisement itself. This will allow your customers to really play the game and grab a bargain for themselves while bringing you plenty of potential prospects.

6. How to Quickly Boost Your Profits with a Business Coach

If your son, daughter or spouse were involved in a car accident and needed specialized attention from a specific type of doctor, would you opt to attempt the surgery yourself in your garage at home? Of course not. It's ridiculous to even suggest such a thing, isn't it? Well, that's how ridiculous it sounds when I hear business owners, who have never even created one single successful advertisement in their twenty years in business, tell me that they refuse to hire marketing consultants.

The unfortunate reality is most business owners know they have major problems with closing ratios, marketing, sales scripts and getting customers into their business. However, they refuse to invest the necessary experts to fix their problems.

After speaking with many business owners, I have found that failure to get expert advice is mostly due to business owners having too much pride to ask for help. Some have never even considered hiring experts in the first place.

If you really want fast results without wasting money researching then trying out different strategies, then hiring an expert marketing consultant to guide you in generating more quality buying customers and converting more leads to sales should be the first thing you do — right after preparing your mindset for accepting success. Until you hire an expert consultant, you have no idea the numerous benefits you will gain with having an expert work with you one-on-one.

With an expert marketing consultant in your business, you will no longer feel alone and isolated from other successful business owners. You will no longer feel the doom and dread of having the weight of your business solely on your shoulders. Most importantly, you will have a support system to give you powerful and proven creative ideas to increase your profits.

Now, when I say expert marketing consultant, I'm not referring to some high-priced advertising agency that has no proven track record of increasing sales and profits in a business like yours. I am also not talking about the yellow page ad reps, radio ad reps or any other type of advertising representative trying to sell you something. I'm talking about a marketing expert who comes into your office, analyses your business with a magnifying glass and then creates custom marketing and sales and tracking strategies tailored for your business — that don't cost you a fortune to use.

PART TWO: STRATEGIES TO GENERATE MORE SALES AND INCREASE PROFITS

7. Customized Promotions & Sales for Every Customer

What if you had the power to look into your customers mind and pinpoint the exact products and services they wanted to buy? How much easier would it be to make huge profits in your business? Well, if you have sold to a customer before, then you already have a glimpse into their wants and needs and you have probably never even realized it.

One of the most under-appreciated strategies that I commonly see business owners neglect to implement in their business is the tracking of customer purchases. If a customer has already purchased pieces of a specific product line or collection, then you know that 99% of the time they will be willing to consider buying similar or complementary products and services. This is one area of your business which can quickly catapult your business profits.

In order for you to use this strategy, you must record orders or generate computerized receipts which give every detail about your customer's purchase. For example, you will want to know the collection name, the exact products or services they purchased, their size, colour and price discounting etc. The best way to use this information is to use a computer program to generate your receipts and track your customer's purchases.

Once you have specific information about a customer's purchase, you can create a promotion or ad every couple of months to generate sales.

Tesco in the USA rolled out this strategy intensively. They looked at their tracked information and realised they didn't really know anything about their customers or their wants. By test-rolling out a loyalty points program, they could aggregate information about customer spending habits and the popular items being sold.

They started out by offering common, high demand items for a discount and displayed them along side complementary (and higher profit) products — then tracked everything. Looking at their data, they could see other opportunities such as offering individuals specialisied discount coupons. These coupons were for other higher profit products customers occasionally bought so Tesco could increase their purchase frequency. Using this collected data, they could also test and tweak other offers to encourage more frequent visits and increased profits. By offering their customers more of what they wanted, they were building a loyalty base very few companies could compete with. Those points created a high level of resistance in visiting a competitors store The higher the points were, the less likely they would switch companies — even if they were offering the same product at a lower price.

While I happened to use Tesco in this example you might have recognised an Australian retailer who duplicated this program on a national scale and who went from rapidly losing market share retailer to one with very strong growth during a recession — Coles.

8. Capture Contact Info & Following Up

We touched on it earlier but this is important enough to go into a little more details. Capturing your prospects contact information when they visit your business, website or call-in, must be the foundation of your business strategies.

This simple concept is powerful, effective and is being used profitability by many well-known businesses. Unfortunately, a lot just don't know how to use this powerful strategy. They allow prospects to wander in and out of their businesses without ever getting their name, email address or phone number.

Which is easier?

To sell someone who has never seen or heard of you before? Or to sell to someone who recently purchased and was happy with the experience and the product? You spent a lot of money getting them to the door and they might not necessarily buy immediately. Let's maximize their value by following up. OK?

The other benefit of capturing your prospects contact information is you gain the peace of mind that comes with being able to generate sales at will.

Following Up:

Let's look at the numbers to see just how profitable this strategy is:

Example 1:

300 leads into your business per month

5% closing ratio = 15 buyers

$500 average sale

300 prospects x 5% closing ratio x $500 average purchase = $7,500 in sales per month.

In the example above you never get a chance to sell to the other 95 prospects because you neglected to get their contact information, so that is a ton of missed opportunity. Now, look at the same example as if you captured their contact information and were able to get another (easy) five percent to come back and purchase from your business with a future compelling sale or promotion.

Example 2:

Assuming that you were only able to get an additional 5% of your prospects to return back into your business and purchase using a follow up campaign:

300 leads into your business per month

10% closing rate (5% initial closing ratio PLUS 5% who buy later from your follow–up campaign = 30 buyers

$500 average sale

300 prospects x 30 buyers x $500 average purchase = $15,000 per month!

Instead of $7,500 in sales you are now making $15,000 in sales! That is an impressive jump in sales that can be achieved by simply by collecting your prospects contact information and then following up by mail, email or phone.

You can see that all you have to do is bring them back into your business and continue closing at the same ratio you already are. You can easily double your sales per month. Now, do you see how powerful and profitable this strategy can be?

Remember when we looked at the cost of bringing a customer into your business, the CPC? By re-contacting the people who didn't immediately buy, we can halve that CPC or even more! Look at the above example and using the $50 CPC from the first Key, by re-contacting just once, we reduced it to $25!

Don't think of stopping at one follow up! We still have 85% who didn't buy yet. It's been scientifically proven time and again that it can take 7 to 10 touches before someone buys from you. We're only on number 2. I know businesses that have follow up systems that never end. That's not a sales funnel - it's a sales funpark! In some industries it can take over 2 years to get a sale but when that sale is worth hundreds of thousands of dollars, you'd be kicking yourself if you didn't follow up forever as well, right?

Just like many of the strategies revealed in this book, you must always be testing conversion systems to consistently and predictably bring customers back into your business to buy from you.

Finally, you may be thinking that prospects are not willing to give you their contact information, but that is not true. The key to getting their contact information is to give them a special offer in exchange for them giving up their contact information. For example, you can offer to mail them out special promotions or offer to enter their name in a free prize give-away. You can even offer to give them a free informative booklet in exchange for their contact information.

Many of the biggest and most successful businesses in the world spend thousands of dollars building a list of prospects that may not be ready to buy from them today, because they know it means millions of dollars in profits in the future when they are ready.

9. OFFERS TO YOUR LIST

One of the easiest strategies is to send targeted offers to your existing customer list. You no longer have to sit on the sidelines day after day while your business has little to no customers or clients walking in the door. You can control your monthly profits with precision simply by just sending out an offer.

"Let's write a swimming pool"

In 1984, during a Playboy interview with John Lennon and Paul McCartney, this exchange occurred. PLAYBOY: Paul, when you and John were still hungry, you'd say to yourselves before composing a song, "Let's write a car. Let's write a house."

PAUL: Yeah. "Let's write a swimming pool."

Do you have old stock sitting around taking up valuable warehouse space? What about out–of–season merchandise that you'd like to swap for something you can make a profit on? By offering them at a discount to your existing customers who know and trust you, you can build goodwill, strengthen the relationship and free up both space and cash you can use for more profitable merchandise... Write your own swimming pool.

Some Ideas on How to prepare the Offer.

The first step is being clear on the offer, the benefits it gives the reader and why you are offering it. The more generous the offer is (right back to wholesale or less!), The more goodwill you bring to the relationship and the faster it sells. Each letter is prepared using mail–merge or similar so that the letter is a personal one directed at them — not a mass mailing.

Next, because we're talking about selling something that might be out of season for a low price, we need to explain that the quality is just as good as before and the only reason you are selling it is to free up the floor space and use the cash on more current in-demand stock. Also explain the reason you are offering it to them first, before it goes on public sale is because you appreciate their business in the past and you want to give back to them.

To sweeten the deal you can also try bundling it with something they would normally buy anyway — both to increase the overall margin for you and to make the offer more enticing to them.

Next we say the inventory is limited and we won't be repeating this offer again (all true). Now give a clear deadline that they need to respond by and how to respond (call, email, fax etc.).

This is the essence of a direct mail letter. For a detailed guide and sample, visit www.MarketingThatWorks.com.au/gifts.

10. INBOUND CALL SCRIPTING

Did you know that you are probably losing a lot of money every single day? By not having a proven and powerful phone answering script that's designed to capture your customers contact information or ask them to make a purchase over the phone — that's how.

Let me prove it to you. When someone calls your business asking for directions to your location, what do you give them? Directions of course. When a customer calls and asks you the price for delivery, what do you give them? Delivery price, of course. Do you know when that person is planning on coming into your business? Do you know if they are even planning to come into your business at all? The answer is probably not.

What if you offered incoming phone call prospects the option to take advantage of the special sale you are having for today only for 5% to 10% off for first-time buyers when they make a purchase, Do you think that would give them an incentive to buy today?

What about offering to put them on a special list for the next big promotions or sale that you are having? Your priorities for every incoming phone call you receive from a prospect should be the following:

- Collect their name, phone and email address so you can add them to your follow-up campaign.

- Record the reason why they are calling as well as the products and services they are interested in — so you know what your marketplace wants.

- If you have a product you can sell, offer them the option to purchase by phone. They might already know what they want.

- Get them to commit to coming into your business today by setting an appointment.

If you are truly seeking profitable success with your incoming phone calls, it is also important that you select and train the best staff person to answer your phone. I am fairly confident that you have someone on your staff that sounds nice, pleasant and professional on the phone and truly enjoys talking to customers.

This is the type of person you want answering your phones on a daily basis. With a proven script, you will be surprised at how many prospects will give you a chance to earn their business simply because someone spoke nicely to them, collected their contact information and set an appointment.

You also will want to train this staff person to follow-up on outgoing calls to prospects and leads that are in your marketing funnel. Sometimes prospects just need to know that someone cares enough about their needs and wants, and someone willing to make a little extra effort. This simple little strategy has paid huge rewards over the years for my clients, and it doesn't cost you one extra cent.

11. Turning Receipts into More Sales

When you go to the grocery business have you ever noticed that your receipts have coupons on them? Some shoppers collect the coupons religiously so they can use them on their next purchase. These coupons are just receipts with an offer printed on them.

This same strategy is often used on Pizza boxes. It works on invoices, bill statements, anything you need to print for the customer.

Have you also noticed that when you go to a fast food restaurant, that they offer to enter your name into a monthly drawing for a prize if you call into a special number and leave your opinion and feedback?

Think about these things from a business point of view. The reason why they use these strategies is because they consistently generate more sales and profits. Whole advertising companies have been built using this strategy for many years because people LOVE coupons and purchasing items that are on sale.

The reason why businesses collect customer opinions and feedback is because it allows them to keep their pulse on the rapid changes in the marketplace and see the areas of their business they need to improve or change.

Still, a lot of businesses have yet to catch onto these profitable strategies. In fact, many business owners in non–retail industries have never considered the possibility of having a mini–ad, discount or coupon printed on their sales receipts. You can even advertise your refer–a–friend rewards program on them.

This transforms a worthless piece of paper into a money–generating magnet, just by making a simple change.

12. TURNING FEEDBACK INTO PROFITS

Feedback from your customers is an important way to understand what you're doing right and wrong in your business. Positive feedback or testimonials should be used everywhere to overcome initial buyer resistance and negative ones should be looked at closely to see what went wrong.

Did you know a lot of people are genuinely reluctant to 'raise a fuss' unless things are really bad? For every person that steps up and leaves negative feedback, 20 others probably didn't bother... They just tell their friends and NEVER come back. Frightening isn't it? Imagine if you never bothered to ask for feedback in the first place.... so listen to them and look closely at the causes to save you a ton of pain in the future.

You should always promote and highlight your customer feedback phone number. For this number, you should use a separate voice mailbox number rather than your business line.

Your customers can then call and leave a message. I also like to offer SMS, QR Codes and in-store feedback card options so I don't miss out on any. Remember the earlier chapter on knowing your customer? How some people prefer newspapers to websites and voice over SMS? The same is true in giving you feedback. Having an option to reply in their comfort zone is critical to getting them to actually do it.

Another sneaky tactic you can use to increase your online testimonials is to use automated feedback services. When someone leaves a review of 4 or 5, they get a response asking if they would like to share that same review online — with a link to your preferred review site pre-filled in. You can quickly improve your online rating and it only takes a couple of extra clicks for the customer.

To set up a voicemail number, just call your phone service provider (or use an online service) and let them know that you want a voicemail only phone number. This extra voicemail phone number may only costs five or ten dollars a month, but the advantage is tremendous.

By using this technique, you discover exactly what your customers want and their view of how their experience went. Once you get the testimonial, you can now use that in all your other advertising to prove to prospects that you are the best option in your market place which provides social proof that you are a leader in your industry. Brilliant.

13. Signs That Sells

Some of the most valuable real estate in your business is your signage. If you have been in business any amount of time, then you already know that good business signage can be critical in helping customers find your business. However, have you ever thought about using business signage to actually attract prospects to your business?

When I talk about business signage, I am referring to signs on the outside of your business windows, as I assume your building signage is already completed and cannot be changed. Most of the window business signs owners use is usually generic stuff like, "Sale," "Financing Terms Available," or "Holiday Sale." In this day and age those types of signs are not worth the plastic they're printed on.

If you really want powerful and effective signs on the windows of your showroom, you must use signs that state your U.S.D. and draw customers in. For example, which one do you think is more powerful: "Sale" or "Guaranteed Same Day Delivery on In-Stock Products or It's FREE!". Or these two: "We Sell All Major Appliances" or "FREE Delivery with Any Purchase Over $500!"

The key to having business signage which triggers prospects and customers to buy is to focus on the benefits that customers want. If you have no idea what the customers in your marketplace are looking for then you need to ask every prospect that comes into your business and use that information to create a U.S.D. that attracts the right type of prospect.

Another place for you to focus on effective business signage that most businesses overlook is inside your business. Just because you got a prospect to walk into your business doesn't mean that your job is done. In your office, store or building, you must have signs that capture the prospects attention and compel them to ask you about it. Here's a quick test you can perform to see if you have good signage in your business:

13. Signs That Sells

When is the last time a customer was in your business and pointed to a sign and asked you about that product/program/service/offer? If the answer is never or you can't remember, then chances are that your in–business signage isn't working as effectively as it could be.

Effective in–business signage can help your staff close a sale, remind customers of why they came into your business in the first place or help close a sale for you because customers are constantly reminded of your unique U.S.D.

14. NEWSLETTERS

Most business owners usually remember to run ads once in a while, but only a select few choose to mail out a quarterly or monthly newsletter to past customers and prospects. This simple little strategy has been collectively responsible for billions of dollars in profits for business owners who choose to actually use this strategy in their business. Those who don't are often left wondering why their customers never come back to buy, even after spending many hours building rapport.

Using monthly or quarterly newsletters can literally mean the difference between struggling to pay your lease or mortgage each month and still making a nice little profit in those dreaded slow months.

No matter how much rapport you may have built with a prospect or customer at the time they were in your office or on the phone with you, the minute they walk out the door, anything and everything is fighting for their attention. They have spouses, children, jobs, relatives, vacations, shopping and bills all fighting for their attention. They may have the best motives and intentions when you talk to them, but the longer you wait to follow up with them, the more they will forget you.

Have you ever run into a prospect or past customer at the grocery business or out and about your local community who you felt should have really come back to buy from you — but when you ask them what happened, they tell you they bought it somewhere else? How did that make you feel? Well, why does that happen? Most of the time it happens because sales people forget to follow up and you don't have a system in place to make sure that the prospects never forget you.

Newsletters are a great way to remind them of you and keep your business in mind.

What to include in a Newsletter.

Your newsletter should contain a paragraph or two on what's happening with you, your family or your staff. People buy from people and people are always curious about other people... Just look at all the 'drama' and 'soap' stories on TV.

Your newsletter doesn't have to be dramatic, just interesting. You can always include the antics of pets and babies... They always generate positive talk.

Include an article or customer interview about how they can do something better, easier, faster or more effectively with whatever that's related to your business.

Finally, drop in a Cross–Word and a Sudoku puzzle — you can find generators online, just search Google then copy and paste...

When it comes to sending your newsletter to your past customers, you should also think about generating referrals and highlighting your loyalty rewards program.

You should also include a unique promotion in your newsletter. Something that rewards your customers for coming back and buying again.

15. OFFERING WORKSHOPS, CLASSES & EVENTS

One of the easiest ways to instantly generate profits and sales is to piggy-back off other successful ideas and strategies. When you ride the back of other successful trends, you eliminate the learning curve and create instant success. Many financial advisors, money managers and even home supply stores like Bunnings and Mitre 10 have been using the strategy of hosting workshops, classes and events for their prospects and customers for many years and it's a big lead generator for them. Many of their classes are booked to capacity and customers and prospects love it.

That's why I highly recommend creating your own type of lead generating and credibility–building workshops. As long as you are creating relevant content that your prospects find valuable, easy to implement and entertaining, you will find this to be a successful strategy.

The first step is deciding how often you want to run your workshops. My advice is to have a workshop at least once per month. This allows your prospects to develop a relationship with you while also building your credibility in the eyes of your marketplace.

Secondly, decide how long you want your workshops to last. The best length for most businesses would range from sixty to ninety minutes.

Once you decide that, then you can begin putting together an outline of the type of information that you would want to give away to your prospects. You can choose from several various formats for your workshop.

Here are some examples:

Question & Answer Sessions

Interview the Expert

Do–It–Yourself

Product Demonstrations

Regardless of the format that you choose, just be sure that the content is relevant, useful and fairly fresh to your marketplace.

After you decide the frequency, length and format of your workshops, the next step is deciding the location and delivery method. There are several different formats you can use to do this depending on your business model. Here are some examples:

Video — Buy an inexpensive video recorder and film yourself doing your workshop. Then, use a service like Youtube.com to post your video to a special page on your website. Remember to advertise your online video workshop in your regular marketing efforts (see part three for another take on this).

In–office/Store/Warehouse/Factory Presentations — This is when you have the prospects come to your business location to listen and watch your informative presentation.

Teleseminars — With this strategy you get a teleconference phone number and have prospects call in on a certain day and time.

Audio CD — You can record your workshop using software on your computer and then burn copies to a disc. Then, mail them out to your list of prospects.

Webinars — You can use a service that records your computer screen while you are talking and showing information via a PowerPoint slide presentation.

It's important to remember that this strategy can only be effective if you advertise them aggressively and if your content is relevant to your marketplace. The other good thing about this strategy is that you can really attract the attention of the local media by submitting regularly scheduled press releases and doing email campaigns and feature spots in your monthly and quarterly newsletters for your workshop, class or event. All in all, you can really generate some massive publicity and quality leads by implementing this strategy.

16. GEO-MAGNETIC LEADS

Whenever someone makes a new purchase, one of the first things they do is brag to their family, friends and neighbours. Your goal in using this strategy is to tap into that excitement and leverage it to create new customers. I like to call this strategy the Geo-magnetic strategy.

By using this strategy, you can capture that excitement and gain access to new customers. Secondly, most people tend to have friends with similar interests who live in the same neighbourhoods. When you have a customer who comes into your business and makes a purchase, chances are that their neighbourhood is filled with other prospects that would also be able to afford and appreciate your products or services.

In order to use this, you simply take the address of a recent customer and draw an imaginary circle around their house which represents an actual distance of five to ten blocks. Once you have your circle drawn, you then mail out a campaign to those prospects inside the circle.

The theme of the campaign is focused around teasing your prospects by revealing that someone in their neighbourhood bought from you, so they should as well. You will also offer them a special neighbourly discount because they happen to live in the same area as the new customer. You can map out the addresses close to your current customer and mail them automatically through online postal services or a third party Mailing Fulfilment Company.

Let's examine a campaign:

When a customer purchases from you, collate or go online and purchase a list of addresses of their neighbours and add them to a spreadsheet (I use a database).

Write, create or purchase a series of three to seven mailers consisting of postcards or letters and a discount coupon for the same or similar product.

Include a unique URL that direct the prospects to a special website page specifically designed for neighbours of the customer.

On the web page you ask that to activate the deal, you need their email address then offer a further incentive to get them to set an appointment to visit your business within a short timeframe.

Using a professional printer or online service you can schedule your series of mailers to go out automatically to the neighbours of your most recent customers.

17. YELLOW PAGES MIGHT STILL BE RELEVANT

In this age of domination by companies that use online marketing, it's hard to imagine that advertising in the yellow pages is still effective, but it is. It seems that everyone is singing the praises of the tremendous impact that marketing on the internet has, but there are still many older prospects that still prefer to use the yellow pages.

These are the people who have spent twenty, thirty or forty years using the Yellow Pages to look up a product or service, so the habit is hard to change.

This strategy highlights the importance of knowing your customer demographics. If they grew up online, you'll likely reach them online. If they grew up reading print or finding business in the yellow pages, you need to be there too.

The yellow pages are especially important when it comes to finding a local service business. The downside of the Internet is that it is sometimes difficult to find a local company because the local company hasn't engaged a professional internet marketer and is competing with millions of other company websites. In those cases, a prospect may start by searching online, but then quickly decides to use the yellow pages because they are practically guaranteed to find a local service provider. This means that you should also continue to use the yellow pages as a place to advertise your business. However, you must create an ad that makes your business stick out and compels the prospect to call or visit your business.

The keys to creating an ad that generates leads and prospects are pretty much the same as I listed in previous chapters:

1. Use headlines that attract customers.

2. Always have a compelling offer.

3. Insert testimonials from past customers.

4. Include a guarantee on your products and services.

5. Your ad must look unique and stand out from your competitors.

6. Your ad must ONLY focus on what your customer wants.

7. Have only one goal for each ad, which is to get customers to visit your business or call.

8. Tell the reason why you're offering the deal.

9. Write ads that are straight to the point and easy to understand. Don't use complicated words or industry jargon.

18. Referral Riches

A Referral Generation Plan is just as important as any other aspect of your marketing system. While every business owner loves to get referrals, very few have a system in place to consistently generate those referrals. As you probably already know, referrals close at a much higher rate than most other types of leads. If you want to take your business to the next level, you should definitely create a system that generates referrals.

There are three steps in an R.G.P. that makes it simple yet powerful.

The first step in creating a powerful R.G.P. is that you have a product or service that is worth referring. It must be memorable and perform exactly as it is supposed to (or better!) in order for your customers to refer their friends and family to your business. If you have a crappy product that doesn't hold up over time or if you have a service that causes more problems than it solves (and I am sure you don't have any of these) then it will be very difficult for the few customers you do get to refer others to you. You don't keep taking a boat onto the water that leaks.

First you find where the leaks are, what needs to be done to fix it and of course, fix them. If your business is leaking cash with poor staff attitudes, forgotten requests or follow-ups, missed appointments etc., well you've got a leaky boat and its best to start there before expecting a referral system to work.

The second step in creating a referral system is to build your request for referrals into your closing process. However, I am not saying that you should ask for referrals before you close the sale. You should ask for referrals after a customer had decided to buy, but before they leave your business. For example, if you are an accountant and you have a client in front of you while you are doing their taxes, then that moment is the perfect time to ask them if they know of anyone who also wants to get their taxes done. If they say yes, you then ask for permission to contact that referral and use the referring person's name. People like to feel good and justify their buying decision. One common way is to tell their friends what a great buy they made.

The last and final component to a successful Referral Generation Plan is to find a way to easily and automatically contact your customers and remind them to send you referrals. The best way that I've discovered to accomplish this is by inserting your customers into a monthly or quarterly mailing campaign that is designed to generate referrals. This can be a series of postcards, letters, emails or phone calls that reminds them that you build your business by getting referrals from customers just like them. Just make sure that whatever method you choose, you do it consistently.

Depending on your customer base, it can be an advantage to add incentives to boost your referral rate by adding a Referral Credit Program. With this program you reward your past customers with business credit for referring someone who purchases over a certain amount to your business and mentions your customer's name as the referring party. If you structure your program this way, your customers will begin to pre-qualify the friends and people that they refer to you.

This is a powerful strategy but only if you are providing a quality product and good service. It's also powerful because you can train your new customers to buy from you in certain dollar amounts to qualify for certain rewards. This allows you to influence their average purchase amount, which then allows you to increase your profits.

It always amazes me that more businesses don't use this strategy. It really is a great program when applied correctly. If you want to take it up a notch then send each one of your customers ten or twenty referral cards that look like business cards and have a blank area for them to write their name and phone number on it. You may also want to include a special discount coupon on the card so that their referral would be sure to give the referring customers' name when visiting your business. This way you train your customers to always be on the lookout for referrals, because it actually pays for them to refer people to you. You may also want to max your referral credits at a specific amount that can be redeemed for each purchase once your program gets rolling along.

Pizza Hut recently used this strategy for their online launch. For every pizza a customer purchased, they gave them a virtual slice to send to a friend. When that friend had four virtual slices, they could redeem them for a pizza purchased online. They gave away a million pizzas, sold five and a half million in a week, built a massive database of pizza customers they can contact forever AND created massive media attention. All for the raw cost of some dough and toppings. Wouldn't you like to grow your business that fast and that cheaply?

19. Bundling For Profits

Most businesses in the retail industry have long profited from this strategy, but most service providers neglect to use this strategy to its fullest potential. Packaging your products and services into bundles allows you to charge higher prices and creating the perception in the market place that you are a premium product or service provider.

The bundling strategy allows you to promote and advertise several other products while initially getting customers to come into your business to purchase other products or services. This dramatically reduces your marketing costs because you are essentially piggy–backing on your current advertising efforts.

For example, if you own a tree–cutting business, then you can offer to cut down one tree for $399 or you can have a package that includes chopping down up to five trees for $999. This package would represent $1,000 in savings for your customers, but it would also allow you to make more profit on every transaction. You could even have a premium package that includes cutting down one tree and landscaping maintenance for one month for $599. In this case, you are already in front of the customer for one service, so why not offer them a valuable package that would entice them to purchase more from you.

The one thing that I would caution you to watch out for with this strategy, is the temptation to lower your prices to the point where you are making peanuts for profits and developing a reputation for being the cheapest company in your industry. Even in the most competitive marketplaces you can package your products and services in a way that will allow you to charge a premium price. Always look to add value to the customer purchase and reward for upgrading rather than reduce or discount your prices. Take the time today to sit down and come up with several different ways you can package your products and services to step your customers up your product or service offerings.

20. THE UP–SELL, CROSS–SELL AND DOWN–SELL

When you get a prospect who says they are ready to purchase do you or your staff hurriedly write up the order and process the payment because you are afraid they will change their mind? How many times have you had someone take the time to visit your business or sit through a sales presentation only to say they want to go and think about it. Well, these are two cases where you have an alternative option that could result in bigger profits.

If you are like most business owners I consult with, then you probably just process the payment when a customer says they want to buy and let a customer walk when they say they want to go home and think about it. However, I guarantee you that if you are doing those two things, then you are missing out on a ton of cash.

The key to turning the regular sale into a spectacular sale is to have an option for the customer to instantly get more/bigger/better at a great value because they are buying right now.

McDonalds are famous for this.

The Up-Sell

"I'd like a Big Mac thanks."

"Have you tried our McAngus. It's 100% Aussie prime Angus Beef that just melts in your mouth topped with a unique tangy BBQ sauce that's to die for. It's available for another week and is only $2 more. Would you like to try it?"

The Cross-Sell

"Would you like fries with that?"

This is a cross-sell because you are adding complementary items from acrosss your range to the sale that increases the size of that order.

The Down-Sell

"Try our loose change menu"

The down–sell is when a client or prospect decides not to buy a specific product or service. In this case, you can offer a scaled down version of the product or service for a cheaper price. This works really well when you attract customers to your business based on a package of products or services and as they raise objections, you can begin to strip the package apart and offer single items or services for a reduced fee. You can still get a sale albeit at a lower profit point AND you have them as a customer that you can market to for life (or at least until they ask you to stop).

There have been companies who have increased the average amount of the order by 50% or more, just by having up–sells and cross–sells.

The 3-Sells system has been proven time and time again to work for thousands of companies who implemented these profit building systems. Now it's time for you to harness the power of these strategies too.

21. Endorsed Offers

Partnering with other businesses to promote your business is a strategy that few business owners ever consider. It's probably because this will require you to be really confident and comfortable in your own business. Otherwise, it would seem like you are risking losing your customers to the other business, but that is not true.

The key to this strategy is partnering with companies that don't sell the same types of products or services that you sell. Just to be clear about this strategy; you will not be exchanging the addresses of your customers with other businesses, you will be creating an in-business coupon or referral program that other businesses will give out to their customers.

When you partner with other businesses who sell complementary products and services to the same target market that you do, it allows you to gain access to your joint venture partner's customers who may be in the market for what you sell. For example, if you are an accountant who finds that working with business owners is your most profitable niche, then you should look to partner with money managers, consultants and marketing firms because they also work with business owners.

Now, when I say partner with these other businesses, what I mean is to work out a mutually beneficial relationship with them. For example, you could host an informative workshop together and both of you send out a mailer to your list of past customers and both of you share the costs of the mailer and event location.

If you are having a problem coming up with some potential joint venture partners, here are a few questions to get the ball rolling:

- What other business or services sell related services to your customers?

- What other related products or services do your customers need that you don't have the ability to sell them?

- What friends or family members do you know that own a business?

- What are some local businesses that you would really like to help succeed.

As part of the endorsement, create a special offer just for their customers. It's a powerful referral when a trusted business recommends you so all care and attention to detail is important. The best businesses to set this up with are businesses such as Layers, Accountants or other service businesses. These types of businesses are where a high level of authority and trust generated between them and their clients. The lower the authoritative relationship, the more your business needs to be sold to get a response.

Commonly, there are four types of endorsed mailings and I'll explain each in order of preference, but first the overall letter should contain the following points:

- Who he is

- Who you are

- How you have helped him

- Why he recommends you

- The exclusive offer and expiry

- How to get it (The call to action)

- The P.S. (Summary of offer and why)

If your endorsing partner is marketing savvy, you should be able to ask for some limited split testing of the letter to his customer base.

The four types are:

1. Direct Mailing

Direct mailing uses an actual letter sent on the endorsing businesses letterhead. It is the most intimate and powerful way to recommend someone (other than in-person).

2. Email

If the endorsing business regularly sends out emails to their list, sending your endorsement as a special emailing works wonders. It's free to send and usually read within a day or two.

3. Flyers

I'm sure you've come across one of these in the past. Billing statements and occasionally bank statements have included a flyer or brochure with an offer from a third party.

4. Free Reports

A free report is simply a short booklet talking about something they can use to improve something they have, enjoy or use.

Let's say that you install home automation equipment. You could create a report talking about the latest smart-phone controlled lighting that can be installed by simply changing a light bulb. At the end of the report you can showcase one or two of the more professional systems that integrate together (which you sell) with your contact details.

If you did a deal with a local hardware (that sells those smart-globes) to include your booklet on how to set it all up with every globe sold, you both win. They get a free guide to encourage more sales and you get access to people who might invariably be disappointed with the limited functionality or who want a more integrated system.

22. Offer Extended Warranty Programs

No matter what product or service that you sell, there is probably a warranty or insurance program you could offer your customers. Selling product or service warranty plans should be a major part of every product business's marketing and training focus. We all know the statistics showing that the large majority of servicing plans are never redeemed, so it is essentially free money for the business owner.

Most business owners I consult with place very little emphasis on using or improving their closing ratio on their warranty plans. If you are serious about capturing your fair share of this free money, spend at least one day a month working on sharing and improving your most successful presentations and scripts for selling your servicing and warranty plans with your staff.

One of the advanced strategies for really maximizing your warranty or insurance plans is to offer your customers who don't opt for the warranty plan (works with anyone really) a gift certificate for an annual (or bi-annual) free product or service inspection. In reality, this offer is an polite reason to 1) Visit them and leave referral coupons, 2) To see if they have any problems with their product and want to get another one at a reduced fee or 3) Sell them something else that goes with the product or service they bought. If they buy a new one, you can trade the old one back and sell it on Gumtree.com.au or eBay as gently used.

The actual cost to you is only the sales person's time and the wholesale price of the goods. When you break these costs down to a monthly fee, you'll be surprised how affordable it sounds.

The key to this strategy is to track what customers have bought and use a follow up sequence so you don't miss a date. You are tracking all your sales aren't you?

PART THREE: ONLINE MARKETING

23. Start with a Website that Actually Generates Sales

Imagine waking up at 7am in the morning and already having sold five thousand dollars' worth of your products through your website. Imagine checking your email after breakfast and finding that you have three appointments that were booked during the night! That's the feeling you can experience on a regular basis once you create an effective website for your business. When I say effective website, I am NOT talking about just having a "pretty brochure" website for your friends and family members to compliment you on. I'm talking about a website that generates leads and automatically transforms visitors into buying customers.

A website that actually generates money may seem like a far-fetched idea for some business owners, but it doesn't have to be a fantasy for you. You must be willing to make a few simple changes though. For most business owners, therein lies the problem. Chances are that you don't have the foggiest idea about what it takes to turn your basic website into a money maker. I am here to give you some direction on the steps you must take in order to transform your website expense into a stream of revenue.

The first component of a successful website is making sure that your website looks professional and clearly shows your products, services, prices, specifications, contact phone number and directions to your business. There is nothing more frustrating than having to search all over a website to find a phone number or office address. If you have a reputable business (and you do!), then you should post as much information on your website about your products and services as possible.

Secondly, your website must have an opt–in form to capture your prospects email address. You have probably seen this email opt–in form on other websites that you frequent. An opt–in form is a place on your website that asks a website visitor for their email address in exchange for something like a free report, discount coupon or newsletter subscription. However, you must offer highly desirable "lead attractant" in exchange for a prospect's email address. You don't attract many Bees with water, you offer them easy to find flowers and in return you can get honey. When it comes to the lead attractant, it's important that your prospects view your offer as valuable and are willing to give you their email address. Your lead attractant can be just about anything related to your business.

Third, your website must have a method to connect with website visitors in a personal way. You can use video, audio or a simple head shot photo on the home page which gives the website visitor a personalized greeting from you. The video can be recorded with a simple digital camera and then uploaded to YouTube.com. Once it's on YouTube, you can then put the video on your website. If you already have a website, you can get your web designer and tech guy to make all of these specific changes.

The fourth change should be making sure you have emails pre–programmed into your website, which are automatically sent out to prospects who signed up to receive your attractant. By pre–programming your emails, it appears as if you are following up with every prospect personally. This will give you the ability to follow up with your leads automatically for as long as you want.

These are just a few of the changes which should be made to your website in order to convert prospects into customers. There are many more changes, but the one principle you need to remember is this: Hire an experienced marketer to design your website to sell. Don't make the mistake of allowing a graphic designer or tech guy (or even a helpful relative - sorry, just saying) design your website without the input and guidance of an experienced marketer. Otherwise, you will have a beautiful website that never makes you a dime.

Advertise Your Website URL on Everything in Your Business

Promoting the heck out of your website is one very effective but underrated online strategy that can have a dramatic impact on your bottom line. As I already established in early chapters, just having a website and putting it online is not enough to get money in your bank account. Many business owners I consult with are under the false impression that having a website is the savior of their business. This couldn't be further from the truth.

In today's technologically advanced culture, having a website is simply mandatory. In fact, you are viewed as a dinosaur if you do not have website. From a customer's perspective, having a website is not seen as a huge advantage. From a customer's perspective every business should have a website.

It's best to view your website as a separate tool that you can use to generate sales. It is not the answer to all your sales woes. After all, it's not the website that sets you apart; it is about your U.S.D. and your ability to consistently attract customers to your website. Once you get prospects to your website, your next job is to actually write words and use images on your website that compel your customer to open their wallet, take out their credit card and purchase from you.

Your website address should be advertised on your business cards, sales receipts, business windows, business signage, and product information spec sheets and anywhere else you can think of. This strategy works even better if you have a memorable website address. For example, if you were a mortgage broker, then consider the following website address: www.GuaranteedLowestInterestRate.com.au. That would at least catch your attention if you saw it and you were in the market for a loan. The important key is to remember that your website does nothing for you unless you get visitors to your website and then are able to convert them into buyers.

24. INCREASING SALES WITH PAY-PER-CLICK

Most business owners realize the benefits of website marketing, but many owners do little to nothing to get their website in front of prospective customers on a consistent basis. Having a website built for your business and getting your website up and running online is only the first step. Your website won't make you one measly sale if you are not able to get it in front of prospective customers.

People who are willing, ready and able to spend money to purchase your products or services.

There are dozens of strategies to generate leads and prospects online, but in the next several chapters, I will cover the most profitable and easy to set up strategies that I have come across in my years of internet marketing.

One of the cheapest and quickest strategies to get up and running is the pay per click strategy or P.P.C. If you haven't heard of pay per click before, then let me give you a brief overview.

When you visit a search engine website like Google and type in a word or phrase and click enter, you will see a webpage which shows the results of the search you entered. On the very top of the page you will see two or three search results that will be highlighted in a shaded box that has a different colour than the rest of the page. On the far right of the webpage you will also notice a row of eight to ten ads. The ads at the top and right of the search results page are ads placed there by companies who pay anywhere from five cents to fifty dollars to show up as an advertiser for a specific word. However, they only pay the fee if a potential customer clicks on the ad.

There is also a bidding component to pay per click, which means that many advertisers are bidding a certain amount to be near the top of the list of advertisers on the search results webpage. The most expensive industries to be using P.P.C. are Lawyers and Insurance.

Using pay per click is such a powerful strategy that many million dollar companies have been built on the back of this one strategy. However, there are several key components to this which must be in place to turn it into a money maker for your business.

The keys to success when using pay per click are:

• Bid in small amounts until you get really good at it.

• Have a compelling ad which attracts the right type of prospective customer.

• Have a special website or page designed specifically for your pay per click campaign. Your normal website will not make you one cent in most cases if you just plug it into your pay per click campaign.

• Hire an expert pay per click manager if you want the best start to your campaigns.

Did you know you can geographically target an area to display your ad in? That is only people searching for your products or services that come from that area will see your ad. Saving you advertising dollars and getting the local customers you want.

25. Writing and Submitting Informative & Educational Articles Online

When customers begin shopping for a new product or service, they often start by finding as much information as possible about vendors, quality and local businesses who can supply them. The number one goal of most customers is to find products or services with decent quality in a price range that they can afford. The only way to locate these products and vendors is to research online before purchasing.

In order to make a good impression on the prospect that is doing their homework, you have to make sure that you are putting your business information in a place where consumers will easily find it. There is no better way to do this than by writing informative and educational articles and having them posted on websites where your target prospects are likely to be searching.

Writing and submitting articles to online directories allows you to really control the flow of information about your products and services in your local market. I have had tremendous success using short articles containing about four to five hundred words to generate leads and prospects. You don't have to be the next Tom Clancy or Stephen King in order to get prospects to read your articles. All you have to do is write a short couple of paragraphs about a particular collection, promotion or sale that you currently are advertising.

The subject of the articles should be educational but also slightly entertaining. The last thing you want to be is boring and sounding like you are writing a user's manual. Consumers want to know that your products, services and business will provide a good quality product that benefits them, but they also like to work with people that are fun, exciting and helpful.

If you are a pretty good writer, you can write your own articles to promote your business, however, I strongly suggest hiring a freelance writer to submit one or two articles per week on your behalf to the top ten or twenty online directories.

Writing and submitting articles to online directories will help to boost your rankings in popular search engines like Google and Yahoo!. These search engines will give your website higher priority when a prospect types in a keyword and will give you a better chance to you to show up as one of the first ten choices in your target market.

Articles (or their excerpts) are more and more commonly being posted on Social media sites such as Facebook, Google+ and Scribd. If that's where your customers are, then that's where you need to be.

26. PARTNERING WITH OTHER WEBSITES

If having a website that actually generates sales is a rare thing for a small to medium business, then partnering with other websites to swap or purchase advertising space must seem next to impossible. Once you have a website that attracts your target customer, then partnering with other websites to help each other generate customers is not that far of a reach.

This is another strategy which seems intimidating on the surface level, but once you get started, it's actually pretty simple.

Obviously this strategy requires that you have a website; however, there is another step you must complete before implementing this strategy.

The first step is having a graphic designer create several various sized web banners for you to market your business on other websites. The next step is making sure that you can actually post ads on your website or get your webmaster or tech guy post them online. Once this step is done, you can them move on to implementing the strategy.

The easiest way to implement this strategy is to start by researching the local businesses that you currently use on an ongoing basis. The first step you should do is visit Google, enter their business name and find out if they even have a website. If they have a website that looks decent then visit their business just like normal and speak to the owner or the person in charge of marketing and introduce yourself. If you are not recognized by anyone, then let them know that you are a regular customer.

Once you have introduced yourself, let them know that you have a website and you would like to do an ad swap with them. Let them know that you will promote their business for free on your website, but you would like free advertising on theirs in return. This should be enough of a hook for a semi–intelligent business owner to move forward with the partnership. If they don't bite on this, then just move on to the next local business that you frequent and make the same offer.

There are two key notes to mention when using this strategy. The first key is make sure you have tracking software installed on your website, so you will know exactly which advertising partner a prospect is coming from. Secondly, make sure the prospect is redirected to a specific webpage that is optimized to sell to these types of customers. Your website manager should know how to do both of these fairly easily.

27. Get Googled

Most of the time, having a beautiful website that highlights your products, services, office and staff is a wonderful and necessary marketing tool. However, you will never make a single cent from your website if prospective customers cannot find your website online.

Every business owners I consult with knows that he needs a website, but virtually none know how to ensure that their prospective customers find their website before finding their competitors. In this chapter I will reveal how you can practically guarantee that your prospects find your website before your competitors.

Having a general idea about how search engines work is the first step in making sure prospects can find your website online. Search engines are websites like Google.com, Yahoo.com and Bing.com. These websites compile tons of data and information on websites like yours and make sifting through it manageable by organizing it in order of importance to the "keyword" you typed into your browser.

For example, if you type in "pizza restaurants in Central Coast, NSW" into your search engine website, then you will get the most relevant pizza restaurants in the Central Coast, NSW that your search engine feels ranks most closely to the phrase or keyword term you typed in. That's why you want your website and the pages on your website to match as closely to the relevant terms that your target market seeks out as possible.

Understanding how prospects search online is the second thing you must understand in order to ensure that prospects find your website. For example, if a customer is looking for a plumber who specializes in working with gold plated piping, then you need to have a webpage on your website that is especially designed for those types of customers. The simplest way to think of this concept is by focusing on "buyer keywords."

Buyer keywords are words that prospects type into their search engine browser to find places to buy the product or service they are looking for. For example, if you were a fashion store owner, who do you think is a more serious prospect: the customer who types in "sofa bed sales for Easter weekend," or the customer who types in "sofa bed"? If you had to choose between designing a webpage on your website for generic sofa beds or designing a specific webpage for sofa bed sales for the Easter weekend, which one should you choose?

Because of the importance of websites being found with search engines, a lot of, let's call them black hat SEO's, have tried to 'game' the system by flooding pages with keywords so they seemed more relevant and hence, got listed first. The search engines know this and have stated quite empathetically that their vision is to find the most relevant and informative sites for the searched for terms. They are constantly tweaking their secret formula to remove the poor content pages and highlight the informative ones.

One way they are doing this is tracking industry specific words and phrases. A plumber website would include the words fittings, taps, pipes, (usually) emergency repairs, service area, business, maintenance etc. Where a plumbing supply company would omit everything not related to the fittings and parts they supply.

Each industry has its own collection of lexical words so it's important that you know what yours are — and use them.

SEO is also inclusive of word–of–mouth — social media. If people are talking about your business favourably (reviews, recommendations etc.), you are more likely to be ranked higher than a business with none or poor reviews.

The number of relevant websites lining back to yours or an article you wrote are also factored into the results. As is website loading speed, ease of use, mobile support and special meta–tagging schemes to allow automatic classification of websites, authors and content.

It seems like a lot (and it is) but it's vitally important that you understand what's involved and either choose to study the intricacies or to hire someone to do it for you. Most business owners don't have the time or the cash to hire someone specifically to do this for them, but prefer to outsource it. You should too.

For more information about SEO, what to look for and how to find an SEO expert who won't use black-hat SEO techniques, risking your website to being banned in google forever, grab my SEO guide at www.MarketingThatWorks.com.au/gifts

28. Harnessing the Power of Classifieds to Boost Profits

In the last decade, customers purchasing products online have accounted for tens of billions of dollars in sales. Millions of those dollars have changed hands as a direct result of having been seen on eBay.com.au. In fact, every month millions of Australians shop online at popular classified websites. One popular strategy for a business that sells a product consists of advertising your entry level, slightly damaged or discontinued products online for reduced prices on Gumtree.com.au and eBay.com.au. This lets you generate profits from a product that traditionally just sits in your warehouse for months or years and collects dust.

The best part about Gumtree.com.au is the fact that it's free to advertise unlimited products on the website. The biggest technical obstacle you will face when advertising on Gumtree is the taking and uploading of images then writing compelling descriptions about the products you are selling. You can have one of your staff members specialize in posting your listings to the website on a daily basis, so you don't personally have to do the work.

You may also want to consider advertising on other online classified websites like Craigslist.com or Kiji.com. These website work much like Gumtree, but they do not get the same local volume of visitors and prospects.

Using these free classified ad websites is a much quicker and profitable way to sell your entry level merchandise and slightly used products than waiting around for the product to become obsolete. You may also want to consider working your new and regular merchandise into your Gumtree marketing strategy.

If you don't mind paying to list your products, eBay.com.au is the biggest and global to boot.

There are some heavy caveats to using eBay.

1) You Must use a PayPal account (owned by ebay).

2) The Buyer is King. Any disputes usually leave the seller out of pocket.

3) Their fee's are higher than normal Credit Card processors.

4) You cannot directly reference your business or website.

Caveat Venditor

Listing Your Business in Highly Visible Online Directories

Have you ever been searching for a product and service online that you felt should have been easy to find, but were unable to find it? How did that make you feel? You probably felt frustrated and maybe even gave up and changed your mind on using the product or service. Well, that's exactly the feeling that you want your prospects to avoid. One of the ways to make sure that this doesn't happen is to make sure your business is listed on every possible online directory.

In order for you to understand the importance of listing your business in all relevant online business directories, you first need to understand how customers may find your business online. See, over the last couple of years, small business owners has been told that prospects no longer use the physical phone book or yellow pages to locate businesses. However, there are some prospects that still check the phone book when looking for certain types of businesses.

The same rule applies when prospects are searching online. While Google, Yahoo and Bing control over 75% of the search engine market, millions of prospect still use online business directories like Yelp, TrueLocal and various other online directories to find consumer friendly business with a track record of quality and high levels of customer service.

In order to find a comprehensive list of online business directories relevent to your industry, visit your preferred search engine and type in the keyphrase "online business directories" and your industry.

29. EMAIL MARKETING

Over the past several years, having a website has become the standard expectation of a successful business. Most business owners have either purchased a website or have a simple web page that directs visitors to their business. However, less than one percent of small to medium businesses utilize effective email marketing campaigns to give their customers incentives to purchase from their businesses after their initial visit to the website or showroom.

Neglecting to implement an effective email marketing campaign is the same as sweeping thousands of dollars into the gutter each month.

Since I've began helping business owners increase their sales and profits, I have discovered the reason why so many business owners miss out on the easy profits from their website. The number one reason for missing out on the easy profits is because most business owners do not actually get their prospects or customers email address. If you never have the email address then you cannot possibly use it to market to your prospects and past customers.

When I say email marketing, I'm not just talking about collecting email addresses of customers who have emailed you with questions, because most times that doesn't really happen. In order to have an effective email marketing campaign, you must have enticing bait that visitor's get in exchange for giving you their email address.

For example, if you were an accountant, your "email attractant" could be a coupon, rewards program or a simple informative report titled, "7 Insider Strategies to Hiring An Accountant" or similar. In order to capture the email address you can one of the services that I recommend by visiting www.MarketingThatWorks.com.au/gifts.

Once you have the email address you can then send emails about sales, promotions or helpful information. You cannot just send out emails begging prospects or customers to buy. Your emails must be fun, educational and timely. Unless you are a professional writer and marketer, you will want to hire one to write your emails and suggest the best frequency to send them out to get the most impact — and profits.

30. Creating A Weekly or Monthly Online Newsletter

If you truly want to explode your profits and sales in your business, then get out of the salesman mentality and get into the relationship building mentality. When you began to see your prospects and customers as people who can become your friends and extended family, you will treat them differently. Many times over the years I have seen customers become irate and cancel orders simply because the salesperson treated them with a cold detached manner, instead of talking to them as a friend. Building relationships with your customers has to be your number one priority if you want to create customers for life.

One of the ways in which you can build a relationship with your prospects and customers is by sending out fun, educational and entertaining newsletters once per month/ quarter. At a minimum you should send out the newsletters once a quarter to your past customers and once a month to your prospects that you've collected email addresses from.

It is very important that the content of your newsletter be natural and not too well polished. In reality, the more down to earth and simple your newsletter is, the more customers will be able to relate to you through your newsletter. In fact, the last thing you want to do is create a slick looking newsletter that uses words, phrases and pictures that are nothing like what you would actually say or do. Remember, this is about building a relationship with YOU and your business. It's not about putting out the most professional newsletter on the planet.

The content of your newsletter should include pictures of you and your staff. You should also include pictures of your customers having fun or purchasing in your business. It is also a good idea to include a contest or sweepstakes which rewards customers for reading the newsletter and answering hidden questions in it. You also want the newsletter to be laid back and not just industry jargon and talk. Most of your customers don't know industry jargon and don't care about it, but they do care about their pets, gardening and recipes. As silly as it sounds, you want your newsletter to be written for the normal guy and gal. Of course, you want to put a section promoting your products and services too, but that should be a small percentage of your newsletter.

31. Social Media

You can't ignore social media for your business. Its growth has outpaced every technological improvement to date and dominates every aspect of our lives.

Facebook alone has over 1.3 Billion active members. There are twice as many people logging into Facebook every day than there are people in the United States! Over 28% of Facebook users even check their news feed before getting out of bed via their mobile! It's staggering to think about isn't it?

People want to feel connected with their friends and family, talk about their lives and share it all with one click. Facebook understands this and is always experimenting new features to simplify and enhance this (along with capturing demographic data to sell to advertisers - us). Did you know that more than 50% of all Australians who have an internet connection have a Facebook account? That's more than one in two of your customers talking to their average of 130 friends every day.

Remember the saying "Good news travels fast, bad news travels faster"? Online, it's not fast. Its exponentially mind boggling fast.

Facebook is an amazing platform to get your message out and engage your customers. Every time someone wants to share a moment with their friends, they can do it in one place just once, and all of their friends see that update and can respond in kind. Think about the power of being able to engage your customers, have them endorse your message and pass it on to hundreds of people just like them...

Be very aware of why people visit Facebook. They are not there to be spammed by your offers. They are there to socialize, see what's going on with their friends and share interesting, funny or inspiring snippets of info. A good general rule is to keep your promotions to around 10% of your postings. As always, feel free to play with the ratios — once your testing has some numbers.

Facebook is free to use, create groups, business pages and especially contact your fans. For a great guide to Marketing with Facebook, visit www.MarketingThatWorks.com.au/gifts. It's free to download and covers everything you need to get started in using Facebook for your business.

There are many other social media sites out there. Google+ is one I recommend you also be a part of. Why? Have you seen the search results with the picture of the author on the left? That is done by putting special meta information inside the web page. The browser doesn't show it but the search engines see it and can use it to display the author of the article as part of the search results. Part of that meta information is a link back to your Google+ profile. I won't go into details here (it's a bit technical and beyond the scope of this book) but everyone who uses content marketing should be adding it to their website.

There are other niched social sites for people to join and if your customers are there, you should be too.

PART FOUR: PUBLICITY STRATEGIES THAT GENERATE HUGE PROFITS FOR LITTLE TO NO COST

32. PRESS RELEASE PROFITS

Although many people don't know it, Press Releases are one of the top marketing tools to get your website not only traffic but popularity as well. For this chapter, I'll go into a little more in depth so you can start using them straight away.

A press release is an announcement of your business event, a new product that will be launching soon or even a new service that you will be offering.

Press releases are much like articles; however a press release is viewed as more newsworthy content rather than informative and educational. Although you can incorporate those two adjectives into press releases as well, the typical press release speaks in a more formal and professional tone.

Press releases can be amazing for your business and your end sales. Although a press release is not meant to sound like a sales promotion, you are however, informing them of a new product or website that will become available soon in the hopes of getting attention for your future launch. Many people don't realize how effective this type of marketing strategy can be for both them and their business.

Press releases also give you instant access to media sites and other news sites such as Yahoo!. Many news sites will scourer press release websites constantly for up–to–date releases so that they can keep adding news related content to their website.

The best part is that your press release now has a chance at being noticed by a ton of potential customers due to the popularity of the large news websites.

Think about it... one of the first things big time movie directors will do before their movie premieres is to hold a huge press conference to get it out to the public. One of the fastest ways to reach out to a ton of people is through the help from the media itself.

The more your press release is out and about, the more of a chance it has at getting noticed and bring your product or websites both visitors and sales.

There are many different aspects when it comes to press releases and their creation. We will talk about helpful websites and services that you can use and how they can be applied to your marketing efforts by attracting future customers.

There will be helpful tips and suggestions the entire way to make sure that you understand the concept and creation portion of your press release. We will also go over the many different options you have for your press release creation whether you decide to do it yourself or have someone else write it for you.

Let's not waste any more time and start learning the right and effective way to making press releases your best friend when it comes to potential sales, traffic, and exposure to tons of viewers daily!

How to Create a Press Release

There are two different ways that you can get a well formatted and high quality press release for your product or business. Creating the press release yourself or having someone else do it for you.

When it comes to creating your own press release there are certain things that you need to know and do before you start. First let's go over some guidelines when it comes to the formatting a press release correctly.

The first thing you need to keep in mind is that in your press release you need to always speak in the third-person. Speaking in the first-person (I) is a big no-no when it comes to creating a press release that will be both effective and keeps your readers reading down the page.

Press releases are meant to be brief — short and to the point. They have a 500 word maximum. Another thing that should go without saying is making sure that you have accurate details in your press release. Remember, this is going out to represent your business. If you get the date or contact number wrong (and I have seen both!), you are not only killing its effectiveness but hurting your reputation and brand!

For the flow of the press release, you want to start out with a luring pre-headline. A pre-headline should be only a single line and is a very short phrase containing only a few words to interest readers to keep on reading.

Examples of these types of headlines are "Coming Soon...", "Secrets Exposed" or "Set for New and Immediate Release..."

After your pre-headline you then want to add an eye catching headline that can ask a question or brings up a problem that someone might be having.

Examples of these types of headlines are, "Do You Really Know Everything There Is to Know about Online Marketing?" or "Who Knew That YouTube's 800,000 Viewers Would Create a Steady Stream of Traffic to Your Website Or Business?"

You want to make sure that you are not sounding too sales oriented in your press release as they are intended on giving someone information and breaking news rather than a sales promotion for your product.

You want your headline to do one major accomplishment for you... Engage the reader to keep on reading. Take time with your headline and think about how you word it.

Tip: I would recommend that you write down as many headlines as you can to describe the core of what they will get, complete the body of the release and then write any more headline ideas that might have come up. Once you have a list, highlight the eye catching ones that create intrigue and ask the people around you to do the same. Taking the most popular couple of headlines, pick the best and keep the others in reserve for the next press release on the same topic.

After your headline, it is time to start composing the body portion of your press release. In the first paragraph you want to inform them about the basics and brief information about your future product launch, business openings, important news or upcoming event.

Although you want to highlight the basics, you don't want to go into detail just yet. Your main goal is to make sure that you give your reader just enough information to keep them reading.

In the next 2–3 paragraphs, you can go into more detail about the topic of your press release. This could include quotes provided by others involved or people associated with your event.

You should also display your 5 W's... Who, What, When, Where, and Why. This is also a good press release format that you can use if you are planning an event or any upcoming company news.

You also want to make sure you are including important keywords that are related to your topic so that when you send your press release to the distributors, it can be easily accessed through search engines with those particular keywords in mind.

Finally, you have the conclusion portion of your press release. In it you want to include a brief summary about your company or organization and a bit of a background when it comes to your knowledge in that particular area.

This will ensure the reader that you are a credible source and lure them into clicking through to wherever it is you want them to go. You can also touch on what you intend to do or goals that you have set for your business and its existence in the online world.

When you create your conclusion, you don't want to drag it out, make sure that you keep your conclusion down to no more than 5 or 6 lines.

After ending your press release you want to make sure that you include all of your contact information so that potential customers and journalists can contact you to ask questions about your press release or about your business.

You also want to include a link to your business website so that potential customers can click through to it and gain a little more information about you, your products, and your business as a whole.

The guidelines listed above will ensure that you have a well formatted and professionally created press release. It is also a good idea to brainstorm your topic before starting. Find the key topics that you will be discussing and make 3–5 points for each sub topic.

After you have created your press release, check for any grammatical or spelling errors. This is a big turn off to readers and will have them clicking off rather than clicking on what you are trying to say. It is always a good idea to hire an editor to check that everything is perfect.

If you still find it difficult to create your very own press release, you can also opt in to a press release writing service. Although they can be a bit pricey, many business owners find it both to be very convenient and well worth the money to get a well written and correctly formatted press release for maximum positive exposure to the media.

We will go over more in detail about some of these specific services a little later.

You can also research online for helpful tips and suggestions to writing a successful press release on your own.

As long as you put your mind to it, you easily can create your very own press release for your business' up-to-date news, future product launches, or events. Here is an example template to get you started in writing your first press release:

—

NEW AND UPCOMING RELEASE...

Date — (Month, Date, and Year)

"This Is Your Headline"

This is your introduction or opening paragraph to your press release. Here's where you briefly introduce the 5 W's of the story. Give it a litle spin to catch their attention.

This is the body. Here you can incorporate the details in the 5 W's — Who, What, When, Where, and Why. Tell them everything they need to know about the news story you're telling — in the order of its importance. Remember to keep it short, no longer than a page and include quotes.

This is your summary or conclusion which is also referred to as a boilerplate. This paragraph should be included at the end of every press release. Tell them a little bit about your company, how long it's been around, who it serves and what it does.

Contact Information:

Your Name

Company Name Cell Number

Email Address

Company Website

—

Get someone else to do it for you

For the many people that don't know the first thing to creating a press release, there are press release writing services available. They can help you with formatting, content, editing and distribution. Of cause, the more services they offer, the pricier they get.

You can shop around and find reasonable prices to have a press release written for your business or upcoming product. A basic press release writing service can cost you anywhere from $100 to even $500.

Many people would rather pay the extra cash to take the task off of their hand because of the way your press release "needs" to be written. A press release, unlike an article needs to be written in a professional tone rather than a friendly tone.

There are a few things you need to keep in mind when it comes to choosing the right press release writing service. Although, there are a ton of good, solid, and reputable press release writing services, there are a dozens more that lack all of these components affecting the quality of your press release.

You want to make sure that the service you choose has good customer feedback and that they provide their customers high quality and unique content for their press release.

You also want to make sure that they are following the same professional format that you want for your press release. Most services will already know the format of an effective press release, however there are imposters that will pose as a press release writer and in the end send you junk!

You should ask them for examples or their work to see that they have the writing skills that you are looking for when it comes to spending your hard earned money.

You will want to send them a copy of the product or detailed information that you want included in your press release. This way, the writing service can grasp a clearer idea of what your product or service is about so they can effectively structure the press release.

You will also want to make sure that they include the keywords that you need sprinkled throughout your press release. This will help in the search engines to drive targeted traffic to you. Good press release distributors rank well in the search engines so when that particular keyword is searched for, your press release will show up and the viewers can click through to your press release.

Explain to the press release writing service that you would like to incorporate keywords throughout your press release and give them a few keywords to use.

Some press release writing services will also include a fee to distribute your press release on many of the press release distribution sites. You would be surprised at how much work this can take off of your shoulders. Many press release services already know the top sources to get your press release noticed, picked up, and published by journalists and news organizations.

This means more traffic heading your way.

The best places to get a press release written is through sites that offer bundle packages which include the actual creation of your press release and a small fee for distribution. Purchasing these services in a bundle saves you a ton of money rather than paying one fee for the creation and a separate (almost as expensive) fee to send it across the web for you.

If you are not familiar with the right places to start posting your press releases to then this could also prove to be a huge time saver by leaving your press release in the hands of experts that do this every day!

Some of the most popular press release writing services advertise on freelancer sites such as Guru.com, Elance.com, and Freelancer.com. Make sure that when you choose an individual that you follow the guidelines and check that they write your press release accordingly.

When you contact a service to create your press release, give them, exactly what you are looking for and your specifics on how you want your press release written. This will lower your chances of getting a bad apple or wasting time.

After you have either created your press release yourself or if you have had a press release writing service create one for you, your next step is distributing it through the internet.

While many of these services can be a bit pricey, they are well worth the investment when you take in effect how much traffic and exposure your press release will get! Let's take a look at some the paid for press release distribution sites.?

Paid For Press Release Distribution Sites

Now that we are ready to send it out, it's time to look at some of the more popular distribution sites like PRWeb.com, PRNewswire.com, and PressReleaseDistribution.net.

Although their rates can be a bit pricey compared to the free methods, they will ensure that your press release is distributed to the harder–to–access news services and are well worth the investment.

PRWeb.com — this has got to be one of the most popular press release distribution sites out on the internet today. They are used by many business owners and they have instant links to big time news sites such as Yahoo! News, Google News, and even MSN.

However, PRWeb.com will only submit your press release to these sites if they give your release a high rating in the way it is written and formatted.

They use a star rating and to ensure that your press release makes it to one of the more popular news websites you have to get a 4 stars or higher. Even if your press release doesn't receive 4 stars, that doesn't mean that it will not be distributed, it will just not be forwarded to the higher value news websites.

Each time a press release is submitted to PRWeb.com, a professional will review the press release and rate it based on the writing, formatting as well as the style of writing used. The higher the rating, the more exposure you will get. PRWeb.com knows their stuff and only hire professionals who know what these news distributors want and they rate yours accordingly. This is why it is so important that your press release is well written!

There are different price ranges for how you want your press release distributed. You should be ready to spend at least $80 to get the exposure you are looking for.

It might seem to be pricy in the beginning but the higher traffic is well worth it in the long run if you want to get noticed!

PRNewswire.com — is another very popular press release distribution site that has over 57 years' experience in this field. In other words, they have connections so you will get the exposure that you are looking for. They also have many different features associated with your account that let you to target your press release campaign and track the numbers as to how well it is doing.

PRNewswire.com is similar to PRWeb.com in that you can be assured that since these are top rated distributors that they are always being looked at by major news sites for the latest news.

PressReleaseDistribution.net — is another widely used press release distribution service that offers 3 different plans to fit your budget. They offer packages as low as $29 and as high as $99.

Each of the plans allow your press release to be disbursed throughout the internet and also give you special features such as email support, a complete status report so that you can monitor your press releases success, as well as allowing you to include your company logo and/or picture.

Your press release will also goes through a review for editing before they submit it to ensure that it is ready to be distributed. They have very good customer feedback and have had great traffic results and, in the end, dynamic sales as well.

Using these sites, the work is basically done for you and will have your press release circulated and returning visitors to your site or product at a very rapid rate.

Many business owners have found this to be a very important marketing tool to get potential customers as well as readers viewing your site and products. The more that your name is out there, the more your products and services are noticed.

Why not start using this tactic today that you will literally be blown away by the results!

You don't always have to pay to have your press release distributed on the web. Many business owners opt to use free press release distribution services. You might not get access to the big names, you still do get a lot of exposure.

Let's take a look at some of the free options...

Free Press Release Distribution Sites

Most of the free press release distribution websites offer the same features as the top rated paid for ones and also allow you to gain media exposure. You won't quite get the exposure that you would if you were a paid for member. However, when you are on a budget and can't afford their services, it is still better to use them than do nothing!

Keep in mind that many of the paid distribution sites also offer free services, they just lack some of the features that a paid member gets.

The same works in the case of free press release distribution sites. They offer upgrades that will give you more features for a fee.

Let's take a look at two of the most popular free sites that give great results, exposure, and cash back in your pocket.

24–7PressRelease.com — this is a very popular free site that has been around since 2004. They give you the option to become a free member as well as upgrades to bigger distribution plans with more exposure. Many people have found 24–7PressRelease.com to be one of the best and most effective free press release distribution sites to get more traffic to your site or product page.

The only downfall to being a free member to 24–7PressRelease is that they have strict guidelines that must be followed before your press release will be published. You can't just create a sloppy press release and expect them to take it for publication, 24–7PressRelease.com's editors will need to approve your press release before they publish it, so it is very important that your press release is structured and formatted the exact way a press release is expected to be.

You will also want to make sure that your press release is free from grammatical and spelling errors as this will hinder your chances of your press release being approved and published on their site.

When you become a free member to 24–7PressRelease. com you are allowed to submit one press release per day for approval and publication. When you are a paid for member you can have multiple press release submissions.

Most likely, if you are just starting out, you will only need to distribute one which makes the free membership enough for your needs. Make sure that you read their guidelines and join today so that you can start submitting immediately!

I–NewsWire.com — is another popular free press release distribution site that has a ton of positive feedback from happy customers that use their free press release services. With I–NewsWire.com you are allowed to submit one press release per week for free. They offer their free members different options to submitting their press release with premium as well as basic features.

The premium features allow your press release to be distributed to 3rd party portals, allows you to display your company logo, will be featured on their home page for 48 hours which increases your link popularity, and many more features for submitting your press release.

The basic features also allow your press release to be distributed, however you will only be able to reach out to a limited amount of viewers.

I–NewsWire.com also has strict guidelines on the formatting and way that your press release is presented so you want to make sure that you read and follow them to a "T" to ensure that your press release is accepted.

I–NewsWire.com also offer upgrade options that give you more features than the free membership. However, the only additional feature you really gain for becoming a paid member is discounts on your distribution plan as well as added graphics, which is why many people go with the free press release submissions at this particular site.

There are a ton of other free press release distribution websites that will allow you to publish your press release and help gain you exposure and traffic. Make sure that you research and find the best free press release website for you and start getting the traffic you need today!

Making The Most Out Of Your Press Release Traffic and SEO

Your main purpose for creating a well formatted and high quality press release is to let everyone know about your new business, product, or service in hopes of generating customers to your products, website, or services.

Press releases are one of the top methods to use to send tons of traffic to wherever it is you want to send them to. That is why it is so important to make sure that your press release is fully geared for the search engines as well.

As we all know, search engines are the number one source for people to find what they are looking for through specific keywords. This is why it is so important for you to incorporate these keywords into your press release for generating traffic back to your website or product.

Using SEO in your press release is much like using it in articles. You want to make sure that you are choosing the right keywords so that your press release can be found. Although much of your traffic will be gained through the help from press release distribution sites, you still need to incorporate SEO into your press release to maximize your chances of it being viewed by the public.

One of the easiest ways in finding out the right keywords for your press release is to do some research using the Google Keyword Tool. This is a very simple and easy tool advertisers use to find out what keywords are being searched for and of course, the most popular keywords that people generally use when searching for your particular niche.

What you want to do is type in your particular niche and click search. You will then see all of the keywords that are related to your niche. Not only can you view how many searches that particular keyword has had for the month, but you can also check to see what the cost per click (CPC — what advertisers are willing to pay per click on their ad) is for that particular keyword and see which keyword is going to generate more viewers.

The more popular a keyword is, the more people are searching for it and the more likely someone is willing to pay top dollar for their ad to get exposure when those words are searched for. This is why it is so important to use those words in your press release — free exposure!

What many people don't realize is how important SEO is to sending traffic to your product or website. Let's face it, search engines rule the web and rather than trying to work against them you'll want to work with them in making sure that viewers get what they are looking for, which might just be your product or website.

Having the right keyword placement throughout your press release will also play a role in your ranking on Google. Like with any other marketing tactic, you want to be on the first page of Google to get the most viewers looking at your press release, which in turn generates more traffic to your website or product.

Although you may not be able to accomplish this your first time around, the more and more you incorporate SEO into your content, the more you will see the search engines working to your advantage.

There are other tools that you can use to find out what keywords are popular in your niche. If you are having a press release created for you by another writer then you will want to make sure that you give them specific keywords to be sprinkled throughout your press release. Doing the research for your writer will help him or her decide how they need to format the press release and how they need to place the keywords in it.

Remember, there is a right way and a wrong way to including keywords in your content which will determine your ranking in a Google search. You want as much exposure to your press release as you can get and including popular keywords is a great way to get more eyes on your press release and ultimately more cash on your wallet.

Ensuring that your press release gets the traffic that you are hoping for plays a big role in whether or not you are able to see sales rolling in. Although you are not trying to sell your product or service through your press release, using keywords will definitely get the viewers that are interested in that particular niche and clicking through to your website or product page.

Keep in mind that a press release is generally a friendly announcement rather than a sales promotion for your product, which means that using popular keywords will help you gain the exposure you are seeking.

You would be surprised to know how many more people become more interested in what you have to say just by adding a few popular and eye catching keywords. Using the right keywords will draw in attention from your audience and entice them to click though just to see what all the fuss is about!

21 Essential Press Release Tips

There are many tips and suggestions available online in regards to a press release. I have compiled a list of some of the most important ones to apply as you create and distribute your press release.

1. Always make sure that you write your press release in 3rd person. Write your press release as if someone else was writing about your business or product.

2. Make sure that you include at least one quote within your press release whether it is a quote from a past customer or from the product or website owner. This will grab the attention of your viewers and will make them keep reading.

3. Make sure that you write your press release with no more than 500 words. Press releases are meant to be short and

sweet and the ideal press release normally ranges from around 250–300 words.

4. Make sure that you are using the searched–for keywords to sprinkle throughout your press release.

5. Include graphics and images to increase the popularity and look of your press release. Many people don't think about the impact that your press release can have on viewers just by adding a simple image, logo, or eye catching graphics.

6. Make sure that you include your URL at the end of your press release. This is a very important key to remember and is your sole way to getting traffic headed over to wherever it is you want them to visit.

7. You can submit your press release to several different distribution sites so that you can really get the exposure that you need for your product or service. The more places your press release can be found, the more you will see your number of visitors increasing and your sales as well.

8. You want to always keep your press release up–to–date and you want to submit them on a regular basis for dynamic results. There is nothing wrong with releasing a press release at least once every few days. The more you have out there that more you will see results out of your efforts.

9. When trying to find the most reliable press release distribution website... do a little testing on your own to find the most effective one. You can do this by alternating which distribution websites you submit your press releases to and tracking the results. Find out which one gives you the most click through ratings and stick with the distribution websites that provide you the best results.

10. If you have never written a press release yourself, take a look at others related to your particular niche for inspiration. You would be surprised at how much you can learn and gain from reading others press releases. Make sure that you are using a press release that is formatted and written correctly. You don't want to be inspired by a press release that will only send you in the wrong direction.

11. Make sure that when you are writing your press release that you use a language that even the most common person can understand and read easily. Realize that not everybody that will be viewing your press release will be a college professor and you don't want to lose viewers just because they don't understand what you are saying or telling them about. Keep your sentences short, avoid three or more syllable words or overly in–industry terms.

12. Spice up your press release by using videos and relevant links. This will not only help the effectiveness of your press release but also draw in more viewers.

13. Check it once, check it twice. Heck, check it three times! You can never review your press release too much and you want your press release perfect! Having even minor grammatical and spelling errors will turn people away and have them clicking off faster than they clicked on it. Try hiring an editor if you struggle with proofreading.

14. Incorporate a little social network marketing with your press release. Using popular social networking sites such as Facebook and Twitter will get the word out to many businesses and people. As we all know the world has turned into a social networking world and what better way to display your press release than from viral sites such as these for added

exposure.

15. Make sure that you are giving helpful information and that you provide a story with your press release. Using a story concept is a great way to lure in readers and hold their attention right to the end of the release. The more attention you have on your press release the better chance you have at them viewing your product or website.

16. Use catchy headlines but don't make them appear like a promotional sales letter... you don't want your viewers thinking that you are trying to sell them, so keep this in mind when thinking of a headline to create for your press release.

17. Make sure that you stay focused on the benefits that come with your advertisement in your press release. Listing benefits is a great plus and adding bullets is an important eye catcher and a way for people to easily recognize the benefits of your product, services, or website.

18. Don't spread hype or provide your readers with fluff. You want to make sure that everything that you say in your press release is as you say it is. Leading your readers to thinking otherwise will not only destroy your reputation but also future sales. For journalists looking to place your press release on their news site, they are looking for real products, websites, and services that give what they say they are going to give. In other words, don't fill their heads with things that you are not providing.

19. Make sure that you provide your readers with contact information. There is nothing worse than reading a press release and finding no contact information. You are basically closing the doors to potential customers and sales. You want to make sure that your readers can easily contact you to ask

you questions or to send their comments, suggestions, or concerns.

20. Try to keep your introduction paragraph as short as possible. Commonly a person will write an introductory paragraph for a press release in as little as 50 words. Remember that your press release needs to be as short and sweet as possible. Make sure that you are able to display all of what you are trying to tell them in as few words as possible while still getting your point across.

21. Make sure that you choose a press release distribution website that allows you to place links to your website. Believe it or not, there are press release distributors that will not allow you to place a link within your press release. Most of the time this only applies with free press release distributions, however, not all free press release distributions have those restrictions, which is why it is very important for you to research and find distributors that allow you to display either you company logo or a link to your website.

Make sure that you follow these simple tips and suggestions the next time you are creating a press release and you will find it simpler and easier to create your very own powerful and attention grabbing one.

A press release can be great to your business as a whole. The only way to truly get your business noticed is by effectively advertising it and what better way to do that than through a press release. Many people don't realize the benefits involved when incorporating press releases into their marketing arsenal.

Press releases reach out to a huge crowd of people which means more potential for your press release to be viewed and of course for future sales. Point blank... you have to get your offer out or no one is going to know about its existence. No matter how well formatted or good your products are, it doesn't make a lick of difference if no one knows about them.

Its OK, not everyone has what it takes to make a compelling yet friendly toned press release, which is why you have many choices when it comes to creating one. Remember that you want your press release perfect and sometimes that means hiring a professional writer to create it for you.

If you find that you enjoy writing press releases for your business, product, or website, then go for it! If you happen to run across problems, questions, or get a little confused about what to say in your press release or how you should format it, you can simply do some research or send me an email.

You can literally find anything you want on the internet today and that includes writing a well formatted and written press release. You can search sites such as Google and YouTube to find helpful tips and advice.

There are also many tools available that will also create a press release for you in simple and easy to use steps.

As long as you use press releases the way that they were intended to be used, you will find that you gain more traffic and sales overall. Many marketers and business owners use this very tactic to gain popularity and traffic to an up-coming product or event and have found it very effective in getting more traffic and sales.

What are you waiting for? Get started and start generating traffic and sales to your website and products with press releases!

33. Be Outrageous: Cashing In On Hot Media Stories

Local residents of Byron Bay were shocked when their local paper ran a front—page story on how residents had spotted the extinct Tasmanian tiger! No one knows for sure whether it was a joke, but one enterprising business owner, Allan Yarrington cashed in and I'll explain how he did and you can too.

What did our smart entrepreneur do? His store wasn't far

from the alleged sightings of the 'tigers' so on the very day the story broke, he had a sign made up and put it by the road near his store. It read:

NEWSFLASH:

Tasmanian Tigers saved from extinction by eating Uncle Tom's Pies.

His claim was that they must have been eating all the leftovers out the back of his store. However, he went even further. He hired three young women and had them pose in front of the sign with tacky feigned looks of horror on their faces. He then called the local paper that ran the story and guess which photo appeared on the front page the following day? The publicity was enormous for little more than a couple of hundred dollars! Everyone in the town was talking and laughing about the whole thing and his business exposure sky-rocketed.

This strategy is a classic 'Publicity Stunt' and it's been used since the days of the late, great P.T Barnham who was a master of raising publicity — outrageously.

The late John Ilham of Crazy Johns used a variation of this. Remember the first renovators TV show 'The Block' where couples competed to have the best renovated house and whoever won, kept the profits? It was filmed in Bondi and the houses were sold at auction on live TV. John had the brilliant idea of having someone dressed as their company mascot go down and buy the best apartment — scoring thousands in free Prime TV publicity throughout the bidding.

What news or events are occurring in your area that you can use to capitalize on?

34. WRITING ARTICLES FOR MAGAZINES AND NEWSPAPERS

The perfect marketing plan should include both paid advertising strategies and free publicity strategies. In fact, free publicity marketing strategies are much more effective in promoting your business than 99% of paid marketing strategies. However, you need both strategies in order to provide a constant stream of growth and profits.

One of the best methods you can use to generate tons of free publicity for your business without coming across as a pushy salesperson, is writing articles for newspapers or magazines. This strategy can pay huge dividends especially when you become as the go-to expert for a publication that your target market reads on a regular basis.

Writing articles for magazines and newspapers not only gets you recognition from your target market, but this strategy also helps you become a magnet for other free publicity opportunities. It is a great feeling to have prospects visit your business and buy from you because you are the expert in your niche. That feeling is a lot different than having people shop your prices all over town, visit your business and receive excellent service from you, but then go and buy from somewhere else because the other business was ten cents cheaper. The best way to avoid being shopped to death is to become the obvious go-to expert for your niche.

The reason why writing articles for magazines and newspapers works so well is because we are all taught from a young age to believe what the newspapers tell us. The majority of people in our culture believe news stories as if they are the gospel. When you become part of the experts that the newspapers and magazines rely on for their information, then you become known as the expert. Your customers will begin to believe everything you tell them as factual and truthful instead of questioning your every little move and decision.

The best way to get your articles included in a newspaper or magazine is to write three to twelve articles and have them professionally edited. You can then contact your local newspaper or target magazines and offer to be a guest writer or offer your articles for inclusion in their publication.

35. SPONSOR LOCAL CHARITY EVENTS

Sponsoring local charity events is another great strategy to build up goodwill towards your business while getting your message across to your target market. Sponsoring local charity events is not a new strategy, but it hasn't really been embraced on a larger scale by many small to medium businesses. However, now that you know about this highly effective strategy, you can reap the rewards of implementing it into your business.

The key to profiting from sponsorship of local charity events is to hone in on your target market and discover what charity events they will be most interested in attending. This requires you to gather information from your target market, which you cannot do unless you ask your customers for their input via your website or with flyers in your business.

Once you gather information from your past and current customers, you can begin to look for sponsorship opportunities that match your target market. There are thousands of sponsorship opportunities right in your local area. The fastest way to find a sponsorship opportunity is to contact non-profit organizations which match your target markets interests.

It is important for you to know that sponsorship opportunities will require an investment from your business ranging from a few hundred dollars to several thousand dollars. Most sponsorship opportunities will have various levels, so don't worry about being locked into a huge expensive contract.

When deciding on a specific non-profit organization or cause to champion, make sure that your business receives maximum coverage on the specific organizations website and marketing material. Remember that the goal of your sponsorship opportunities is to bring exposure to your businesses. However, you can choose a charity event that has significance to you, but just make sure that it serves dual purposes, otherwise it will make you feel really good, but won't generate the desired amount of publicity for your business.

The most critical point in using this strategy is to **promote a compelling offer!** Your name on a shirt or banner isn't enough to guarantee a return on your investment.

36. Start Your Own Blog

Most business owners are content to simply have a nice website, but super-successful small to medium businesses know that they may need something more for their online strategies to be successful. That's when having a blog becomes a necessity.

A blog is a website that allows you to add text, video or pictures instantly without needing to know computer coding or hiring tech guys to reprogram your website.

Websites like Wordpress.com and Blogger.com will give you a free blog space and will walk you through the set up process.

One of the great features of having a blog is your ability to post content online, therefore communicating with your target market with no expensive advertising or marketing costs. Blogs also have a feature which allows your visitors to post comments and text, videos or pictures of their own. This allows you to build a relationship of communication with your target prospects. Of course, this comes with some risk. If you have a prospect or customer who is not happy with your company, product or service, then your blog may serve as a most convenient place for them to voice all of their disapproval.

The best benefit of having a blog is the ability to plug into other popular "social media" websites which are heavily visited by internet users in every target market in the world. Social media websites are websites where the visitors and users have the ability to interact with each other and create online groups or communities of individuals of similar interests.

The success of most strategies such as this one, hinge on your ability to know your target market and create content, products and services which will entice your ideal customer to visit your blog and ultimately, choose your business for their product or service.

37. Guest Blogger On Local Blogs & Websites

Being a guest blogger on other local blogs and websites is one of the more advanced and effective online strategies. This is one step away from being a true joint venture strategy, but it is equally as effective when done properly. In fairness, this strategy does require that you be a decent writer and have the ability to "write on demand". If your writing skills are not up to par, you can always hire a writer to ghost write short articles for you and then post those articles on other blogs.

The huge benefit of this strategy is your implied positioning as the go-to expert to your target market, simply because you are the author of an informative and educational blog posting. In order to make this happen, you must partner with blogs and websites which cater to your target market.

The best way to discover who your target market really is, is to review your previous customer receipts or order forms and compile the information into a spreadsheet or computer document. Once you have the information into a easily understandable format, you can then analyze the data to see specific patterns and trends.

Your next step is to find customers, friends or family members who match the same target demographic as your past customers. Ask them for recommendations of websites and blogs which they frequently visit. You may get lucky and be able to be a featured guest blogger on one of the websites they mention or you may have to find similar websites in your local target market. In either case, your business will benefit from you being viewed as a source of credible information about your products and services.

Once you find websites or blogs that match your target market, there are several ways to contact the blog authors and owners. The first method is a little more stealthy, but basically you just post comments on their blog for a couple of weeks and then email them to let them know that you have written a couple of articles which would make a very good blog posting for that specific niche. It's important that you don't come across as a salesperson for your business or a specific product, but as an author you is willing to provide some informative blog postings to share with their audience.

The second way to contact blog authors and owners is to email them and ask directly if you could be a guest blogger. You will have to email them a copy of your articles that you have written or have paid to have written for you. Once they see that you are serious about giving them good information to post on their blogs, you will definitely have a better chance of becoming a regular guest blogger.

All of these articles should end with an authors bio describing who you are, your interests and website. This is how you bring them back to you.

38. BE A RADIO SHOW GUEST ON LOCAL STATIONS

An effective strategy which attracts customers by the carloads is to become a local celebrity. One of the fastest ways to become well known in a marketplace is to be everywhere your target market hangs out or shops at. Radio is a large proportion of media consumption. In the car, waiting rooms, business work areas.

You can quickly build your celebrity status is to become a regular guest on the local radio circuit. Very few business owners have ever considered being a radio guest as a way to connect with their prospects and customers while growing their business.

The reason why being a radio show guest is so effective is because radio show hosts have already taken the time to build relationships with their listeners and you can piggy back off of their success. The truth of the matter is that every radio station needs guests to fill their airtime for their audience.

The first step in this process is to figure out the radio programs that your prospects listen to on a regular basis. You can do this by asking your customers and prospects with a survey on your website or in your business. You can reward them for providing the information by giving them a coupon for a discount.

Once you have that information, you should begin to listen to those specific radio stations for at least a week or more. Listening to the station will provide you with the general flow and outline of the best programming on that station. After you get a good feel for a station, you can then begin to come up with an interesting angle or story hook to get their attention.

When you have your story angle or hook, hire a writer to write a press release around your idea. You can hire a pretty good writer from websites like Cragislist.com or Getafreelancer.com.

The writer should also be able to send your press releases to your target radio shows at least once or twice each month for a monthly retainer fee (See the earlier Press Release Profits chapter). Your press release will also give the radio station your contact information and story idea.

If the radio station chooses your story idea they will contact you for more information. Of course, your ultimate goal is to be invited to be a guest for one of their shows.

Being a radio show guest does require some skills which you will have to develop in order to be a good guest. For example, you must be entertaining, educational and quick on your feet. It's very much like working with a customer in your office or business, except that you will be speaking into microphone.

There are several programs online which instruct you on how to be a radio show guest that you may want to invest in before implementing this strategy into your business.

39. Start Your Own Internet Radio Show

Admittedly, this is an advanced strategy, but if you have the willingness to learn new things, then you can implement this into your business and make huge profits from the fame.

While advertising on the radio can be profitable, it can become extremely expensive if you try to increase your marketing campaign too quickly. There is a way to avoid those costs altogether, and become famous too. For the smart business owner, a far reaching free publicity strategy is an internet radio show. This may come as a total shock to you, but there are internet radio websites which allow you to start your own show for free. Websites like Blogtalkradio.com and Shoutcast.com allow anyone who has a computer and microphone to create their own radio show. This means you can become an overnight star if you have the talent and ability to put together a program and event on a fairly consistent basis.

The benefit of starting your own internet radio show is that you do not have to pay for radio air–time and you can create and air a show as often as you like. You also benefit because you are the one calling the shots and writing the content for your show. This means that you can make it as commercial as you desire, unlike some of the free publicity strategies.

When creating your own radio show, you can schedule the programming to be as long or as short as you see fit. For example, you can create a one hour show which airs once per week or more. You can also script the show to include guest speakers or just simply be built around your business. It is in your best interest to create a show that is informative and entertaining because your prospects always trying to escape the dull, boring hum of everyday life. If your show can provide that entertainment, then your show will practically be guaranteed to succeed.

The real worth of this strategy is in your ability to get an audience filled with your target market. One of the best ways to do this is by posting a link to your radio show on your own website and on the website of your joint venture partners. You can also post advertisements to your radio show on various other online websites where your target market hangs out.

40. Start Your Own Internet TV Show

Video marketing is the future of online marketing strategies. It's also one of the most advanced strategies for small to medium business owners. The real power of video marketing is its ability to connect your audience to you emotionally and visually. When done correctly, video marketing can reach thousands of prospects in your target market for little to no money out of pocket.

One of the most successful I've come across is Gary Vaynerchuk's Wine Library TV. Gary started out reviewing a selection of wines from his families store, giving honest feedback both good and bad and helped people pair wines with different foods. It grew quickly and added millions to the businesses bottom line. People connected with Gary and chose to order from him — even across the country, when the same wine could be bought from the local store. It obviously wasn't about the price but about the relationship he built with his audience — one video at a time.

How can you turn a commodity into a unique distinction that massively boosts sales in only 10–15 minutes every few days? You don't even have to spend this long on each video. Just 3–4 minutes has been proven effective when you deliver useful information to your audience.

This strategy involves recording a short video with a simple hand held video recorder (or smartphone) and uploading it — all without actually leaving your business. You can even use this video to introduce a specific topic and then have the customers view the remainder of the information from your website. The best part about video marketing is that you can post your video on popular websites like Youtube.com and begin funneling its visitors back to your own website.

But what do you talk about? How-to's are the most popular but anything to increase the viewer understands and knowledge related to your industry will work. People always want to save money, know more, impress their peers at the next BBQ and make informed decisions when they spend their money. How can you help them do it?

While video marketing will require you to have some basic knowledge of camera's and computer software, the benefits far outweigh the learning curve. In fact, you can spend as little as two or three hours getting familiar with the equipment and then begin profiting from this strategy. In my opinion, the best type of video recorder to get you started is the Kodak ZI8 video recorder, which costs less than one hundred dollars, has a microphone input, and shoots pretty decent footage. You can then record yourself presenting a specific product and give your prospects a live tour of the collection.

Using video to describe your products and services, in addition to your normal online guides allows your customers to know what you can do, build a personal relationship with you and make you the authority.

41. Write a Book That Positions You as the Go–To Expert in Your Niche

One of the least used secrets of building a business that is recession proof is establishing yourself as the go–to expert for your industry. One of the best ways I know to accomplish this is by writing a book especially for your target market.

Every business owner loves to find the easy customer who is ready to buy the instant they walk through the door. However, the large majority of customers need days and weeks of gathering information before they make that decision. If you can find a way to become a part of your prospects decision making process when they are searching for information, you will become the expert they learn to rely on. Once you become their familiar expert, the price haggling stops and prospects call or come into your business ready to purchase on your terms.

One of the fastest ways to build instant credibility with your target market is to write a book. Writing a book to educate and help your target market, automatically gives you a huge advantage over your competitors. While your competitors are wasting thousands of dollars relying on newspaper, radio and television ads that are no longer as effective, you will be quietly building yourself a loyal following of premium customers. Prospects, who actually care about reputable businesses and well-known owners, are the kind of quality buyers you can build your business on.

Writing a book also has many other side benefits, just like many of the other strategies I've revealed to you. For starters, local media outlets love business owners who publish books and educational materials for the local market. Secondly, you also gain the fame and celebrity status in your marketplace which brings you other opportunities because you have done something that most other business owners refuse to invest the time to do.

When it comes down to actually writing your book, you can hire a ghostwriter to write a two hundred page book or you can spend a couple of months writing it yourself. A ghostwriter is a writer that you would hire to write a book that you would have exclusive rights in saying that you are the author. In my opinion, if you are looking to hire a ghostwriter, you are better off hiring one who knows your industry and you can reap the benefits of being a published author in a matter of weeks instead of months or years while you personally write your book. Once your book is written, you can easily self-publish it using any number of online services which provide that option. For a guide on self-publishing your book, visit www.MarketingThatWorks.com.au/gifts.

PART FIVE: PAID ADVERTISING STRATEGIES WITH POTENTIAL FOR GREAT RETURNS ON YOUR INVESTMENT

42. Newspaper Advertising

With the invention of the internet, businesses who invest in newspaper advertising has taken a huge nosedive. However, when done correctly, newspaper advertising can still be very profitable for businesses. There are still millions of Australians who faithfully read the newspaper and continue to be exposed to ads each and every day of the week. In the advertising age which we live in, your marketing message must be much more appealing to generate the type of buzz that could have been generated ten years ago with the same type of ad.

The caveat with advertising in the newspaper for most businesses is the inability of advertisers to create ads which actually attract the target prospect and compels them to take action. When you are spending thousand dollars per month on advertising in local newspapers, you need to make sure that your target market is not only seeing your ads, but also responding by coming into your business and purchasing.

Writing and creating newspaper ads requires the skill of an experienced marketer and writer. Sadly, if you think that the ad representative from the newspaper, who receives a commission from selling you that advertising space is the best person to design and create your newspaper marketing campaign, you are in for a long and expensive ride. If you remember nothing else I have written in this book, remember to hire an experienced direct response writer and marketing expert to create ALL of your ads, email's and marketing materials.

The ads you place in your local newspaper should have a headline and content which cause your ideal prospects to immediately grab the phone, visit a website or rush into your business and sign–up for your marketing list or purchase your product or service. If you are running ads and you are seeing little to no action from them, then you are not creating ads which resonate with your target market.

43. How to Create Profitable Radio Commercials

When done correctly, radio commercials can have a tremendous profitable impact on your business. However, very similar to newspaper advertising, there is a skill required to create ads and promotional offers which coax prospects to your website or into your business to make buying decisions.

With radio, you have a chance to make a personal connection with your prospects by using your voice. Prospects will hear your voice and marketing message and can determine for themselves if you sound warm and inviting or cold and forceful like a pushy salesman. If you were one of the one percent of the population who was born with the natural ability to sound like a used car salesman, or even if you are not, then you will definitely need to hire the local radio station talent to record your marketing message. Otherwise record your commercials in your own voice.

Writing and recording radio commercials that generate profits is much like creating any other type of marketing campaign. In fact, you should design your radio commercial by using your existing successful ads which you are using in other parts of your business and use those advertising pieces to provide your content for speaking. If you have done your job correctly, your marketing message and U.S.D. should be identical.

One of the drawbacks of using radio is the restriction on the length of your advertising space. In most cases you will be dealing with fifteen or thirty seconds spots. Shorter advertising spaces mean that your marketing message will have to be clear and to the point. Additionally, you should absolutely use a different website or phone number to track your incoming calls from each and every radio station you are investing in for your business.

Remember, passion sells. If you do not believe in what you are promoting and can't passionately describe it, then please, hire someone who can. I'm not talking about hype. I am talking about a deep-seated belief in what you are saying is true.

44. THE SECRET TO CREATING PROFITABLE TELEVISION COMMERCIALS

Advertising on television is the Holy Grail for most small to medium businesses. However, unless a television commercial is scripted and recorded in a certain manner, it will most certainly be a waste of money. Very much like radio advertising, television ads which include the owners, staff and actual customers will give prospects a revealing look inside the minds of the owners, and should match the image you want to communicate about your business.

Most small business owners think they do not have budget to advertise on television so they never even attempt to explore this strategy. In today's economy, there are several ad agencies which would allow independent retailers to purchase television spots for little to no money at all. Advertising on television has several requirements which will enhance it's success — if followed carefully.

The first requirement is to understand and know your target market. If you haven't taken the time or resources to clearly define your target market and that it is reachable through TV at a certain time or show, you will be needlessly wasting tons of money on television advertising.

The second requirement to television advertising is you must work with an ad agency that can negotiate the price of your airtime in bundles with other local businesses. This will allow you to get much better pricing than if you went to a television station directly. When I say bundles, I don't mean a package of ad spots some good, some not so good or some at 2am! I mean ads at the right time to reach your audience.

When it comes to producing your commercial, if you work with a local television studio, you will be expected to spend anywhere from twenty five hundred dollars to five thousand dollars per thirty second commercial. However, if you really want a huge production with tons of special effects, then expect to spend much more money than that.

At the end of the day, all advertising is a gamble the first time you try it. If you can't afford to lose it - Don't do it!

45. Advertising in Your Local Coupon Booklets

When it comes to inexpensive marketing ideas with potential for maximum profits, advertising in local coupon booklets is near the top of the list. Coupon booklets have the ability to generate tremendous profits because prospects are already looking through the book because they want a bargain. Therefore, placing your advertisements in the book puts your products and services directly in the path of potential buyers.

When advertising in coupon booklets, testing shows that the most effective strategy requires that you create an actual coupon for your prospects.

Many times when browsing through coupon booklets I see advertisers who have nice little ads, but neglect to include a dashed-line box for their coupon that customers bring into their business to get the offer.There might not be much space available to get your message across in a coupon but don't let that stop you from using them.

When you include a coupon with your advertising you are better able to track your results to know which coupon gave you the best return on your investment. You may also want to consider a special website or web page just for your coupon prospects. Having this special website allows you to know the impact your marketing efforts are having in driving traffic to your offer.

At the risk of sounding like a broken record, knowing and truly understanding your target market pays huge dividends when it comes to creating any sort of advertising.

If you know what you target market really desires. In fact, it makes it easier to create ads. With the proper information in your hand, you can create headlines and promotions which specifically motivate your target market to take immediate action.

46. The Awesome Power of Posters, Leaflets and Flyer Inserts

Sometimes the simplest things can lead to success. That's the best way to describe the positive effect that a properly prepared marketing campaign which includes posters, leaflets and flyers, can have on your business.

In most neighbourhoods and communities there are spaces reserved in highly visible areas, which allow flyers and posters to notify residents of upcoming local events. Usually the areas that towns and neighbourhoods reserve for hanging posters and leaflets are also a high-traffic area meaning you can really benefit from an effective poster or leaflets.

You can even use posters on the front of your business windows to drive traffic to your website or into your business. However the overall success of your poster, leaflet and flyer campaign will be dependent on your ability to create an irresistible event. The promotional event you create for your posters and leaflet campaign must have more than just discounts. You should also consider special packaging or giving away free items in exchange for people buying specific dollar amounts.

Another powerful way to use flyers and inserts is to contact your local newspapers and have them distributed in the weekly freebie newspapers as inserts. This ensures that you reach every household in a specific area and usually the pricing for this service is very reasonable.

47. Maximise Profits with Magazine Advertising

While I'm a huge fan of free publicity marketing strategies, you must have a balanced marketing plan. Advertising in local magazines is not only an effective marketing strategy, but you will be better able to predict your leads, customers and overall return on investment consistently when using paid advertising strategies like this one.

This is especially true when you have a proven ad that can bring you consistent results. When you are investing in advertising strategies for magazines, you should only be using an ad that is a proven winner.

It's worth repeating myself here in saying that you must know your target market. If they don't read your selected magazine, you'll just be throwing good money down the drain.

Advertising space in magazines is more expensive than advertising in newspapers. You need to have a pretty good idea that your promotion is effective and has the ability to get you results before you invest the money in this strategy.

There are some tricks to creating effective magazine ads, but the principles which govern successful advertising still apply. For example, you will need a headline which draws attention from your target market and presents a compelling benefit or reason for the prospect to continue reading the rest of your ad.

When you get into investing larger amounts into your advertising, the tracking system that you use becomes even more important, because you will want to instantly know the return on your investment. Keep in mind that your tracking system can be a coupon that the customer has to bring into your business or simply a special website which they can use to purchase the product online.

When advertising in magazines, be prepared to spend some extra cash on top–notch design work as well. Magazines tend to be sticklers about the level of professionalism they want to communicate to their readers and subscribers. The perfect situation is for you to have a partnership with a local designer, who will create all of your ads for you.

Alternatively (and one which I prefer), you can create Advertorials. They are simply ads that look like articles. Using your direct mailing type of copywriting, create an article explaining the benefits of your product and how to get it.

FINALLY

I want to congratulate you on reading this far. This shows your willingness and openness to new ideas and you are ready for success. There is a lot to take in so please, don't be overwhelmed and try to do them all at once. Start at the beginning and work your way through. Even if you only implement a couple of ideas for now, they will put you in step for a more profitable future. While every strategy won't be a good fit for where your business is right now, keep them in mind so that as you grow, you can look at the others and see how adding them will magnify your results.

Where to Start

You can start with the 5 keys followed by creating your ABS Plan. Do each in turn and you will understand your business and customers better. You might even be surprised! There are many examples of businesses who have started down one path and by engaging the customer, discovered what they wanted was far different to what they had imagined for them in the first place.

I know you'll enjoy your business more, get more time to spend with your kids while increasing your profits with the secrets of marketing that works exposed in your hands. Enjoy.

If you have further questions or would like additional ideas or concepts (that are too numerous to fit into one book!), you can contact me at www.MagneticCashflow.com.au.

Warmly,

Michael X. Branson

Index

Symbols

A

O

P

www.ingramcontent.com/pod-product-compliance
Lightning Source LLC
Chambersburg PA
CBHW071221290326
41931CB00037B/1600